FREE Study Skills DVD Offer

Dear Customer,

Thank you for your purchase from Mometrix! We consider it an honor and privilege that you have purchased our product and want to ensure your satisfaction.

As a way of showing our appreciation and to help us better serve you, we have developed a Study Skills DVD that we would like to give you for <u>FREE</u>. **This DVD covers our "best practices" for studying for your exam, from how to use our study materials to how to prepare for the day of the test.**

All that we ask is that you email us your feedback that would describe your experience so far with our product. Good, bad or indifferent, we want to know what you think!

To get your **FREE Study Skills DVD**, email <u>freedvd@mometrix.com</u> with "FREE STUDY SKILLS DVD" in the subject line and the following information in the body of the email:

    a. The name of the product you purchased.

    b. Your product rating on a scale of 1-5, with 5 being the highest rating.

    c. Your feedback. It can be long, short, or anything in-between, just your impressions and experience so far with our product. Good feedback might include how our study material met your needs and will highlight features of the product that you found helpful.

    d. Your full name and shipping address where you would like us to send your free DVD.

If you have any questions or concerns, please don't hesitate to contact me directly.

Thanks again!

Sincerely,

Jay Willis
Vice President of Sales
<u>jay.willis@mometrix.com</u>
1-800-673-8175

Table of Contents

Practice Test #1

Practice Questions

Mathematics

1. $\frac{2x^2 + x - 6}{x+2} =$
   a. (2x-6)
   b. (2x-3)
   c. (2x-2)
   d. (2x+2)

2. Factor the equation $12x^4 - 27x^3 + 6x^2$.
   a. $3x^2(4x - 1)(x - 2)$
   b. $3x^2(4x - 1)(x + 2)$
   c. $3x^2(4x + 1)(x - 2)$
   d. $3x^2(4x - 2)(x - 1)$

3. Find the distance between points P (-3, 4) and Q (1, 6).
   a. $2\sqrt{2}$
   b. $2\sqrt{3}$
   c. $2\sqrt{5}$
   d. $3\sqrt{2}$

4. Which of the following expressions is equivalent to $(3x^{-2})^3$?
   a. $9x^{-6}$
   b. $9x^6$
   c. $27x^{-6}$
   d. $27x^{-4}$

5. If the two lines 2x + y= 0 and y=3 are plotted on a typical *xy* coordinate grid, at which point will they intersect?
   a. -1.5, 3
   b. 1.5, 3
   c. -1.5, 0
   d. 4,1

6. Which of the following expressions is equivalent to $3\left(\frac{6x-3}{3}\right) - 3(9x + 9)$?
   a. -3(7x+10)
   b. -3x +6
   c. (x+3)(x-3)
   d. $3x^2 - 9$

- 4 -

7. Evaluate the expression $(x - 2y)^2$ where x = 3 and y = 2.
   a. -1
   b. +1
   c. +4
   d. -2

8. Given the equation, $\frac{3}{y-5} = \frac{15}{y+4}$ what is the value of y?
   a. 45
   b. 54
   c. $\frac{29}{4}$
   d. $\frac{4}{29}$

9.

y	-4	31	4	68	12
x	-2	3	0	4	2

Which of the following equations satisfies the five sets of numbers shown in the above table?
   a. $y = 2x^2 + 1$
   b. $y = x^3 + 4$
   c. y =2x
   d. y =3x + 1

10. Which of the following is equivalent to the expression $3x + 5y - (2y - 7x)$?
   a. $-4x + 3y$
   b. $-4x - 7y$
   c. $10x - 3y$
   d. $10x + 3y$

11. Which of the following is the sum of the polynomials $5x^2 - 4x + 1$ and $-3x^2 + x - 3$?
   a. $8x^2 - 5x - 2$
   b. $2x^2 + 3x + 2$
   c. $2x^2 - 3x - 2$
   d. $-8x^2 - 3x - 2$

12. Which of the following expressions is a factor of the polynomial $x^2 - 4x - 21$?
   a. $(x - 4)$
   b. $(x - 3)$
   c. $(x + 7)$
   d. $(x - 7)$

13. Which of the following is equivalent to $27x^3 + y^3$?
   a. $(3x + y)(3x + y)(3x + y)$
   b. $(3x + y)(9x^2 - 3xy + y^2)$
   c. $(3x - y)(9x^2 + 3xy + y^2)$
   d. $(3x - y)(9x^2 + 9xy + y^2)$

14. Which of the following expressions is equivalent to $(x - 3)^2$?
   a. $x^2 - 3x + 9$
   b. $x^2 - 6x - 9$
   c. $x^2 - 6x + 9$
   d. $x^2 + 3x - 9$

15. What are the zeros of a quadratic expression, represented by the factors, $(x + 6)$ and $(x - 7)$?
   a. $x = 6$ and $x = 7$
   b. $x = 6$ and $x = -7$
   c. $x = -6$ and $x = 7$
   d. $x = -6$ and $x = -7$

16. Which of the following represents the product of $(4x^3 - 2x + 4)(x - 8)$?
   a. $4x^4 - 32x^3 + 18x - 32$
   b. $4x^4 - 32x^3 - 18x^2 - 2x - 12$
   c. $4x^4 - 32x^3 - 2x^2 + 20x - 32$
   d. $4x^4 - 28x^3 - 2x^2 + 16x - 4$

17. Which of the following represents the difference of $(3x^3 - 9x^2 + 6x) - (8x^3 + 4x^2 - 3x)$?
   a. $-5x^3 - 13x^2 + 9x$
   b. $11x^3 - 13x^2 + 3x$
   c. $-5x^3 - 5x^2 + 3x$
   d. $5x^3 + 13x^2 + 9x$

18. Which of the following represents the correct expansion of $(a + b)^4$?
   a. $a^4 + 3a^3b + 3ab^3 + b^4$
   b. $a^4 + 6a^3b + 4a^2b^2 + 6ab^3 + b^4$
   c. $a^4 + 2a^3b + 4a^2b^2 + 2ab^3 + b^4$
   d. $a^4 + 4a^3b + 6a^2b^2 + 4ab^3 + b^4$

19. Which of the following represents the sum of $\frac{3}{x+2} + \frac{x}{x^2+10x+16}$?
   a. $\frac{3}{x+2}$
   b. $\frac{x+6}{x+8}$
   c. $\frac{2(x+6)}{(x+2)(x+8)}$
   d. $\frac{4(x+6)}{(x+8)(x+2)}$

20. What is the solution to the equation, $\frac{x}{x-6} + \frac{1}{2} = \frac{6}{x-6}$?
   a. $x = 3$
   b. $x = 6$
   c. $x = 9$
   d. No solution

21. Given the expression, $(2^3 + 4^3)$, which of the following expressions is equivalent?
    a. $(2 + 4)(2^2 - (2)(4) + 4^2)$
    b. $(2 + 4)(2 - 4)$
    c. $(2 - 4)(2^2 + (2)(4) + 4^2)$
    d. $(2 - 4)(2^2 - 4^2)$

22. Which of the following represents the factors of the expression, $x^2 + 3x - 28$?
    a. $(x - 14)(x + 2)$
    b. $(x + 6)(x - 3)$
    c. $(x + 4)(x - 1)$
    d. $(x - 4)(x + 7)$

23. Find the midpoint between $-30 + 15i$ and $12 - 3i$.
    a. $9 + 6i$
    b. $-9 + 6i$
    c. $-21 + 9i$
    d. $-24 + 13.5i$

24. Find the distance, rounded to the nearest integer, between $-30 + 15i$ and $12 - 3i$.
    a. 22
    b. 44
    c. 46
    d. 51

25. 60 is 30% of (?)
    a. 90
    b. 180
    c. 200
    d. 210

26. If 40% of x=18, what is x?
    a. 36
    b. 360
    c. 45
    d. 450

27. Which number is 300% of the difference between 23 and 27?
    a. 4
    b. 75
    c. 12
    d. 25

28. What is the simplest form of the following polynomial?
$$4x^3 + x - x^3 + 2x^2 + 3 - 3x^3 + x - 2x^2 - 1$$
    a. $2x + 2$
    b. $x + 1$
    c. $x^3 + 1$
    d. $2(x + 1)$

29. Line M contains the following two points: (1, 10) and (6, 20). What is the slope of line M?
   a. 5
   b. 2
   c. 0.5
   d. 10

30. $p(y) = \frac{4y}{2} + 5$. If $y = 4$, then what is the value of $p(y)$?
   a. 9
   b. 7
   c. 13
   d. 37

Reading

Reading:

Read each passage carefully. Since the assessment is not timed, take as much time as you need to read each passage. Each passage may have one or more questions.

A helpful strategy is to focus on the opening and ending sentences of each paragraph to identify the main idea. Another strategy is to look for key words or phrases within the passage that indicate the author's purpose or the meaning.

Reading Sample Questions:

Read the selection and answer the questions that follow.

How to Choose and Purchase an Automobile

Choosing and purchasing an automobile in a volatile market is not simply a function of color or engine preference; on the contrary, consumers need to treat the purchase of an automobile as the investment that it is—they need to research the pros and cons of owning various automobiles, and they need to make an informed decision before arriving at the dealership. Failure to properly prepare for such an investment can result in an unnecessary economic loss for the consumer.

While there are many pros and cons associated with automobile ownership, many consumers do not adequately research the specifics benefits and <u>detriments</u> associated with purchasing a particular vehicle. One of the most common concerns is economic: how much does it cost to own a particular vehicle over time? The cost of ownership is not limited to purchase price; it also includes things like insurance prices, repair costs, and gas-consumption. While a given vehicle may have a higher sticker price, its low cost of ownership may, over time, offset this expense. Conversely, a vehicle may have a low sticker price but a high cost of ownership over time. Accordingly, consumers should thoroughly research vehicles before they visit an automobile dealership.

There are numerous ways for consumers to research the cost (defined broadly) of a vehicle before they ever step inside that vehicle. Most simply, there are a number of publications that list the relative depreciations of automobiles over time. Consumers can use these publications to track how a particular model tends to lose value over time and choose that vehicle that best retains its value. Consumers can also go directly to a manufacturer's websites to compare gas mileage or the cost of replacement parts. Furthermore, insurance agents can provide insurance quotes for customers before a purchase is made. Awareness of factors such as these can also simplify the purchasing process.

When a consumer is finally ready to purchase a vehicle, he or she is less likely to be pressured by a salesperson if he or she is equipped with the relevant data for that purchase; i.e., if a consumer knows the long-term costs of a particular vehicle, he or she is less likely to be swayed by short-term or cosmetic benefits. Arriving at a dealership unprepared can result in an impulse purchase which, in turn, may result in increased automotive expenditure over time. Conducting even a modicum of research, however, can potentially save the average automotive consumer thousands of dollars in the long-run.

1. Why should consumers treat an automobile purchase as an investment?
    a. Automotive stock is traded on various stock exchanges.
    b. If consumers do not treat it as an investment, they may unnecessarily lose money.
    c. Vehicles may appreciate over time.
    d. Owning a vehicle has potential risks and rewards.

2. Based on the passage, which of the following is another word for the underlined word "detriments?"
    a. purchases
    b. cons
    c. benefits
    d. investments

3. According to the passage, which of the following is true?
    a. Vehicles with a higher sticker price always cost the most over time.
    b. SUV's are always expensive to own.
    c. Red automobiles are more expensive because their insurance rates are higher.
    d. Sticker price does not determine the overall cost of a vehicle.

4. What does the cost of ownership of a vehicle include?
    a. purchase price
    b. gas consumption
    c. cost of repairs
    d. All of the above.

5. If a consumer conducts research before going to an automobile dealership, he or she is:
    a. more likely to be swayed by high-pressure sales techniques.
    b. less likely to be swayed by the short-term benefits associated with a particular vehicle.
    c. more likely to be dismissive with, or rude to, salespeople.
    d. less likely to be concerned with insurance rates associated with a particular vehicle.

6. According to the passage, what information can consumers find on a manufacturer's website that can help them make a sound financial decision?
    a. The gas mileage of a particular vehicle.
    b. The different colors offered for a particular vehicle.
    c. The cost of replacement parts.
    d. A and C

Questions 7-11 pertain to the following passage:
School Days
      As Bill lumbered up the stairs to Hendrickson Hall he wondered if he was up to this—twenty years was a long time, and maybe he had forgotten the ropes. He wasn't even sure if this was the right building.
      "Uh, hey, uh...is this where the Biology labs are?" stammered Bill to a young woman clad all in black. "She's probably an art student," thought Bill.
      "No. This is, like, Hendrickson Hall. You know...the English building."

Bill neither appreciated the girl's eye-rolling nor the snooty way she emphasized "English." Nevertheless, he mumbled a "thank-you" and hurried towards the student center to check his schedule and the campus map.

"Martha, if you weren't gone, you'd be able to show me around this campus lickety-split. You'd probably say, 'Bill, you big dope, can't you find your way around a simple college? What would you do without me?'" Now that she was gone, Bill could answer such questions: Without Martha, he made do. He neither succeeded nor failed; he simply made do.

As he approached the student center doors, a group of cheerleaders approached from inside the center. Without hesitation, Bill opened a door for them and stepped to the side. Ten young, attractive, laughing girls passed through the door without glancing at Bill. He felt like he should be angry or indignant, but instead, he was <u>dumbfounded</u>. He simply could not understand how one person would not think to thank, let alone acknowledge, another person who had done them a good turn. He stood there for about two minutes, silently holding the door, looking back and forth between the center and the direction of the parking lot. Bill gently closed the door, put his hands in his pockets, and began the long walk back to his car.

"I'm sorry Martha, but I can't do it. Things are just too different now. Don't be disappointed; I'll still find things to do. God, I miss you."

7. Based on the passage, exactly how old is Bill?
   a. twenty years old
   b. forty years old
   c. fifty years old
   d. The passage does not state Bill's age.

8. Which of the following best describes Bill's state of mind in the passage?
   a. apathetic
   b. reflective
   c. angry
   d. confused

9. It is most reasonable to assume that Martha:
   a. left Bill for another man.
   b. died suddenly.
   c. is no longer in Bill's life.
   d. is waiting at home for Bill.

10. Which of the following is another word for the underlined word "dumbfounded"?
    a. perplexed
    b. rationalized
    c. dilapidated
    d. entreated

11. Based on the passage, it is reasonable to assume that:
    a. Bill was once a car mechanic.
    b. Bill is a retired college professor.
    c. Bill will not return to college.
    d. Bill never really loved Martha.

Questions 12-17 pertain to the following passage:

Reduction

Reducing liquids is a fundamental culinary skill that any aspiring chef or cook must include in his or her repertoire. A reduction, in short, is a process whereby a given liquid is slowly simmered until its volume diminishes. This diminution causes the flavors of the reduced liquid to intensify and sometimes sweeten. The ability to perform effective reductions is integral because recipes ranging from simple sauces to desserts may call for reductions. Learning how to perform a reduction is perhaps best demonstrated through the classic reduction called for in the recipe for chicken Marsala.

Prior to making the Marsala reduction in a chicken Marsala dish, one should dredge thin chicken breasts in flour and fry the breasts over medium heat until browned. Once the chicken has been browned, remove the chicken and set it aside. Two tablespoons of butter should be melted over medium heat in the same pan in which the chicken was browned. When the butter is melted, one cup of Marsala wine should be added to pan and heated until simmering (lightly boiling). The wine and butter should be allowed to boil down from approximately one cup to approximately one-half cup. When the sauce has reduced, one-half cup of chicken stock and the browned chicken breasts should be added to the mixture. The sauce should be brought back to a simmer and reduced by half (this should take approximately ten to fifteen minutes). When the sauce has reduced by half, it should be thick enough to adhere to the chicken. At this point, it is ready to serve.

The reduction that occurs in the above chicken Marsala recipe is fairly typical of reductions. Whether one is reducing the volume of chicken stock for a soup, or reducing balsamic vinegar or wine, the procedure is essentially the same: simmer the liquid until its volume reduces to the point where it changes the sauce's consistency. While reductions are fairly straightforward, there are some pitfalls in the process. One common mistake that people make is over boiling the sauce. If a sauce is boiled too vigorously it may scorch, which will impart a burnt, acrid taste to the sauce. Another common mistake is adding thickening agents to the sauce because the reduction is not occurring fast enough. Adding starches to the sauce to force it to thicken it will not bring out the same intensity of flavor that a reduction produces. It may also make the final sauce thick and lumpy. The process for making a reduction is simple, but it must be followed closely if one wants his or her sauce to be palatable.

12. The underlined word, diminution, most closely means:
    a. process.
    b. liquid.
    c. decrease.
    d. skill.

13. According to the passage, why is the ability to perform reductions important for chefs or cooks?
    a. The ability to perform reductions demonstrates culinary skill.
    b. Restaurant customers like reductions.
    c. Reductions are popular in contemporary cuisine.
    d. Many recipes call for reductions.

14. In the chicken Marsala recipe, when should butter be added to the pan?
    a. Before the chicken breasts are browned.
    b. After the chicken breasts are browned.
    c. After the wine has begun to simmer.
    d. While the chicken breasts are being browned.

15. At what point does reduction occur in the chicken Marsala recipe?
    a. When the Marsala wine is reduced in half.
    b. When the butter is melted.
    c. When the wine/chicken stock mixture is reduced in half.
    d. At points A and C.

16. Which of the following is a common mistake made when performing reductions?
    a. under boiling the sauce
    b. adding butter
    c. using starches to thicken the sauce
    d. All of the above.

17. What function does the chicken Marsala recipe serve in the passage?
    a. It illustrates the importance of reductions.
    b. It is an example that demonstrates how to do a reduction.
    c. It is an example that demonstrates how not to do a reduction.
    d. It helps the reader relate his or her experience to the passage.

Questions 18-23 pertain to the following passage:
The Grieving Process
Since its formulation, Dr. Kubler-Ross' stages of grieving have been an invaluable tool in understanding how people cope with loss. Although individuals may experience the stages of grieving in varying degrees and in various progressions, the average person tends to go through the following stages when grieving: denial, anger, bargaining, depression, and acceptance. While most of these stages seem natural, many people do not understand the importance of the anger stage in the grieving process.

When a person experiences a significant loss in his or her life, experiencing anger as a result of this loss is both <u>cathartic</u> and therapeutic; in other words, anger at one's loss provides an emotional release and allows for the beginning of the healing process. By directing one's anger at a deity, fate, or even oneself, grieving people can come to realize that tragedies are seldom the fault of an individual or a higher power; rather, loss is a natural part of living that each person must experience. Trying to assign blame can allow the grieving individual to abandon his or her anger by showing that there is no-one to whom blame can be assigned. Having no-one to blame allows the bereaved to begin to heal because he or she can begin to come to terms with the necessity of loss. If an individual cannot move beyond anger, however, he or she may exhibit destructive tendencies.

There are a number of ways that people can fail to properly go through the anger stage of the grieving process. Some individuals may never find an object for their anger. These people may feel a vague, continual irritability or may react unreasonably to circumstances. Other grieving individuals may assign blame to an object but not realize that a given person or entity is blameless. This may result in a loss of religious faith, an unreasonable hatred of an individual, or even self-

- 13 -

destructive tendencies in those individuals who blame themselves. These and other destructive consequences may be avoided if the bereaved successfully negotiate the grieving process.

Anger is not generally approved of in contemporary society because it is associated with violence, hatred, and destruction. Anger does, however, have its place—it is a natural and healthy step in the grieving process. Without experiencing this vital stage, it is difficult, if not impossible, to begin to move past tragedy.

18. Which of the following is true according to the passage?
    a. Grieving individuals can be self-destructive.
    b. Grieving individuals need therapy.
    c. People who suffer tragedy never fully heal.
    d. Crying is a natural consequence of loss.

19. What is the main idea of the first paragraph?
    a. Depression is a normal and important part of the grieving process.
    b. No-one grieves in the same way.
    c. Not moving through the anger stage of the grieving process can produce destructive consequences.
    d. Many people do not understand the importance of anger to the grieving process.

20. Based on the passage, the underlined word, "cathartic," most likely means:
    a. having to do with anger
    b. unhealthy
    c. healthy
    d. related to emotional release

21. How does anger help individuals heal?
    a. It allows the bereaved to more quickly enter into the "bargaining" stage of the grieving process.
    b. It helps people understand that tragedy is usually blameless.
    c. It helps people to lash out at others.
    d. Anger raises immune-responses to infection.

22. Why is anger not generally approved of in contemporary society?
    a. Anger does not serve any positive purpose.
    b. Anger makes people nervous.
    c. Angry people are unpleasant.
    d. Anger is associated with violence, hatred, and destruction.

23. Which of the following are possible consequences of failing to go through the anger stage of the grieving process?
    a. Vague, continued irritability.
    b. The loss of religious faith.
    c. Self-destructive tendencies.
    d. All of the above.

Questions 24-30 pertain to the following passage:

The Coins of Ancient Greece

We don't usually think of coins as works of art, and most of them really do not invite us to do so. The study of coins, their development and history, is termed *numismatics*. Numismatics is a topic of great interest to archeologists and anthropologists, but not usually from the perspective of visual delectation. The coin is intended, after all, to be a utilitarian object, not an artistic one. Many early Greek coins are aesthetically pleasing as well as utilitarian, however, and not simply because they are the earliest examples of the coin design. Rather, Greek civic individualism provides the reason. Every Greek political entity expressed its identity through its coinage.

The idea of stamping metal pellets of a standard weight with an identifying design had its origin on the Ionian Peninsula around 600 B.C. Each of the Greek city-states produced its own coinage adorned with its particular symbols. The designs were changed frequently to commemorate battles, treaties, and other significant occasions. In addition to their primary use as a pragmatic means of facilitating commerce, Greek coins were clearly an expression of civic pride. The popularity of early coinage led to a constant demand for new designs, such that there arose a class of highly skilled artisans who took great pride in their work, so much so that they sometimes even signed it. As a result, Greek coins provide us not only with an invaluable source of historical knowledge, but also with a genuine expression of the evolving Greek sense of form, as well. These minuscule works reflect the development of Greek sculpture from the sixth to the second century B.C. as dependably as do larger works made of marble or other metals. And since they are stamped with the place and date of their production, they provide an historic record of artistic development that is remarkably dependable and complete.

24. What is the purpose of this passage?
   a. To attract new adherents to numismatics as a pastime.
   b. To show how ancient Greeks used coins in commerce.
   c. To teach the reader that money was invented in Greece.
   d. To describe ancient Greek coinage as an art form

25. What is a synonym for "delectation", as used in the third sentence?
   a. Savoring
   b. Choosing
   c. Deciding
   d. Refusing

26. What is meant by the term numismatics?
   a. The study of numbers
   b. Egyptian history
   c. Greek history
   d. The study of coins

27. What is meant by the term *pragmatic*, as used in the third sentence of the second paragraph?
    a. Valuable
    b. Monetary
    c. Useful
    d. Practical

28. Why is it significant that new coin designs were required frequently?
    a. This indicates that there was a lot of commercial activity going on.
    b. This gave the designers a lot of practice.
    c. There were a lot of things to commemorate.
    d. The Greeks needed to find new sources of precious metals.

29. According to the text, how do ancient Greek coins differ from most other coinage?
    a. Simply because they were the first coins.
    b. Each political entity made its own coins.
    c. They were made of precious metals.
    d. They were designed with extraordinary care.

30. What is meant by the phrase "most of them do not invite us to do so", as used in the first sentence?
    a. Money is not usually included when sending an invitation.
    b. Most coins are not particularly attractive.
    c. Invitations are not generally engraved onto coins.
    d. Coins do not speak.

Writing

Read the selection and answer the questions 1-5.

(1) The Freedom Trail is in Boston, Massachusetts and it's a two and a half mile path through the center of Boston that takes you past buildings and places that were important in Boston's history and in Revolutionary War history.
(2) The trail begins on the Boston Common, which is a big park with baseball fields and large grassy stretches. (3) Back in 1634 when it was first established, the Boston Common was usually used to keep livestock like cows. (4) Later, it was a place where soldiers camped out when they passed through the city.
(5) A bit down from the Boston Common is the New State House, which was built in 1798, over 150 years after the Boston Common. (6) Paul Revere helped to decorate the State House by laying copper over the wood. (7) The Old State House, which gave its name to the new one, is located a few blocks away.
(8) The Granary Burying Ground is another spot on the Freedom Trail and is famous because many revolutionary figures are buried in it. (9) The Granary was first used as a cemetary in 1660 and got its name because it was next to a grain storage building. (10) The burying ground has 2,345 markers or gravestones, but some people think that up to 8,000 people are buried in it. (11) Some of the most famous people resting at the Granary are Benjamin Franklin's parents, John Hancock, Paul Revere, and victims of the Boston Massacre.
(12) Further down the Freedom Trail is Faneuil Hall, which was built in 1742. (13) It was built to be an indoor marketplace and is still used as a market today. (14) The second floor of the building was used as a meeting hall, and was used for many famous meetings and gatherings during revolutionary times. (15) Protesters met at Faneuil Hall when they wanted to protest against laws like the Stamp Act and Townshend Act.
(16) Down in Boston's North End stands Paul Revere's house and the famous Old North Church that helped Paul Revere learn that the British troops were coming across the Charles River. (17) After Paul Revere saw the lanterns, he set off on his famous ride.
(18) One of the most famous battles in the Revolutionary War was the Battle of Bunker Hill. (19) The American colonists lost this bloody battle, but their near success taught them that they did have a chance against the British. (20) The Bunker Hill Monument is a tall, white obelisk that looks similar to the Washington Memorial in Washington, D.C., and was another stop on the Freedom Trail.
(21) The last stop on the Freedom Trail is the USS Constitution, which is a warship that was called Old Ironsides during the War of 1812. (22) Paul Revere had his hand in this ship as well because he created the copper fastenings on the ship.
(23) These are just a few of the stops on the Freedom Trail which is a great way for families to learn about the Revolutionary War and colonial times together. (24) Visit the Freedom Trail if you literally want to walk through history!

1. Which change should be made to sentence 1?
    a. Add a comma after *Massachusetts*
    b. Change *it's* to *its*
    c. Add a comma after *buildings*
    d. Add a comma after *Boston's history*

2. What change should be made to sentence 3?
   a. Change 1634 to sixteen-thirty-four
   b. Add a comma after 1634
   c. Change first to 1st
   d. Change usually to unusually

3. What's the most effective way to revise sentence 7?
   a. Because there is an Old State House a few blocks away, the New State House got its name
   b. The Old State House, located a few blocks away, got its name from the New State House
   c. A few blocks away from the New State House is the Old State House, which lent its name to the new State House
   d. The New State House got its name because there is an Old State House a few blocks away

4. What change should be made to sentence 9?
   a. Change cemetary to cemetery.
   b. Add a comma after 1660.
   c. Change its to it's.
   d. Add a comma after grain.

5. What's the most effective way, if any, to revise sentence 11?
   a. Resting at the Granary are some of the most famous people like Benjamin Franklin's parents, John Hancock, Paul Revere, and victims of the Boston Massacre.
   b. Benjamin Franklin's parents, John Hancock, Paul Revere, and victims of the Boston Massacre are resting at the Granary, which has some of the most famous people.
   c. Some of the most famous people, like Benjamin Franklin's parents, John Hancock, Paul Revere, and victims of the Boston Massacre are resting at the Granary.
   d. No change.

6. Which of the following is the best way to write the sentence?
   a. Any person who uses his or her cell phone in a movie theater has little respect for the other audience members.
   b. Any person who uses their cell phone in a movie theater has little respect for the other audience members.
   c. Any person who uses its cell phone in a movie theater has little respect for the other audience members.
   d. Any person who uses his cell phone in a movie theater has little respect for the other audience members.

7. Which of the following versions of the sentence is written correctly?
   a. To repeat ideas in an essay unnecessarily is to commit the mistake of redundant.
   b. To repeat ideas in an essay unnecessarily is to commit the mistake of redundantly.
   c. To repeat ideas in an essay unnecessarily is to commit the mistake of redundancy.
   d. To repeat ideas in an essay unnecessarily is to commit the mistake of redundance.

8. Which version of the sentence is written correctly?
    a. We stopped for extended visits in Indiana, Kansas, Nevada and California during our cross country trip.
    b. We stopped for extended visits, in Indiana, Kansas, Nevada and California during our cross-country trip.
    c. We stopped for extended visits in Indiana, Kansas, Nevada and California, during our cross-country trip.
    d. We stopped for extended visits in Indiana, Kansas, Nevada, and California during our cross-country trip.

9. Which version of the sentence does NOT contain any misspelled words?
    a. I gave my condolence to Juan, whose dog recently ran away from home.
    b. I gave my condolance to Juan, whose dog recently ran away from home.
    c. I gave my condolense to Juan, whose dog recently ran away from home.
    d. I gave my condolanse to Juan, whose dog recently ran away from home.

10. Which version of the sentence does NOT contain any misspelled words?
    a. The suspect remained detained while the police conducted their inquisiton.
    b. The suspect remained detained while the police conducted their inquasition.
    c. The suspect remained detained while the police conducted their inquesition.
    d. The suspect remained detained while the police conducted their inquisition.

11. Which version of the sentence is written correctly?
    a. The two-year-old was just learning how to walk.
    b. The two-year old was just learning how to walk.
    c. The two year-old was just learning how to walk.
    d. The two year old was just learning how to walk.

12. Choose the word that correctly fills the blank the following sentence:
Joanne still needs to finish her homework: revise her essay, _____ the next chapter, and complete the math problems.
    a. reading
    b. to read
    c. read
    d. will read

13. Choose the correct spelling of the word that completes the following sentence:
The black mangrove tree is native, or _____, to South Florida.
    a. indigenous
    b. endigenous
    c. indegenous
    d. endeginous

14. Choose the word that best fills the blank the following sentence:
Peter is so talented with horses that the skittish colt became _____ once Peter took over his training.
    a. frantic
    b. docile
    c. lucid
    d. prudent

15. Choose the words that best fill the blanks in the following sentence:
King George III was _____ to have the American colonists _____ taxes to Britain on luxury items such as tea and paper.
    a. devious, remand
    b. prudent, attribute
    c. detrimental, tribute
    d. determined, pay

16. Choose the words that best fill the blanks in the following sentence:
Susan B. Anthony was _____ that women were _____ the same rights as men, such as equal pay and the right to vote.
    a. glad, written
    b. outraged, denied
    c. determined, have
    d. credulous, given

17. The immigration officer gave Maria's passport a cursory examination before quickly moving on to the next person in line.
What does the word **cursory** mean in this sentence?
    a. Lazy
    b. Angry
    c. Hasty
    d. Careful

18. Choose the word set that best fills the blanks in the following sentence:
As a student council _____, Travis endeavored to _____ his peers to the best of his ability.
    a. represent, representational
    b. representative, represent
    c. representation, represent
    d. represent, representative

19. Identify the figure of speech used in the following sentence:
It was time to go home; the trees waved a fond farewell to speed us on our way.
    a. Irony
    b. Hyperbole
    c. Personification
    d. Euphemism

20. Choose the words that best fill the blanks in the following sentence:
Harper Lee wrote *To Kill a Mockingbird* as an _____ of social _____.
    a. argument, dance
    b. incident, class
    c. exposé, injustice
    d. ulterior, inequalities

21. Which of the following versions of the sentence is written correctly?

    a. Because she wanted to reduce unnecessary waste, Cicily decided to have the television repaired instead of buying a new one.

    b., Cicily decided to have the television repaired because she wanted to reduce unnecessary waste instead of buying a new one.

    c. Cicily decided to have, because she wanted to reduce unnecessary waste, the television repaired instead of buying a new one.

    d. Because Cicily decided to have the television repaired instead of buying a new one she wanted to reduce unnecessary waste.

22. The melody in that pop song is reminiscent of the one Beethoven used in the first movement of his ninth symphony?

Based on how it is used in the sentence, the word <u>reminiscent</u> means

    a. superior
    b. suggestive
    c. situated
    d. synonymous

23. As used in the sentence, "Julie and I made tentative plans to go to the park because she might have to study that day," what does the word <u>tentative</u> mean?

    a. specific
    b. uncertain
    c. absolute
    d. unlikely

24. Although the street could not be seen through them, sunshine still flowed through the translucent curtains.

Based on how it is used in the sentence, the word translucent means

    a. flimsy
    b. transitory
    c. semi-transparent
    d. opaque

25. Which version of the sentence is written correctly?

    a. Veronica was contemptible of the noisy construction workers who made it hard to concentrate on her work.

    b. Veronica was contemptuous of the noisy construction workers who made it hard to concentrate on her work.

    c. Veronica was contempt of the noisy construction workers who made it hard to concentrate on her work.

    d. Veronica was contemptful of the noisy construction workers who made it hard to concentrate on her work.

26. According to Merriam-Webster's Dictionary, which word derives from the English word fawney, which was a gilded brass ring?

    a. fawning
    b. phone
    c. phony
    d. fallen

27. Choose the correct spelling of the word that fills the blank in the following sentence:
Plastic trash that ends up in the ocean can have a _____, or harmful, effect on marine life.
    a. diliterious
    b. deleterious
    c. delaterious
    d. dilaterious

28. Which of the following sentences is correct?
    a. Jason love candy including: lollipops, chocolate bars, and gumdrops.
    b. Jason love candy except: lollipops, chocolate bars, and gumdrops.
    c. Jason love candy, for example: lollipops, chocolate bars, and gumdrops.
    d. Jason loves candy: lollipops, chocolate bars, and gumdrops.

29. Choose the word that best fills the blank in the following sentence:
The selection of the winning lottery numbers is entirely _____ with numbers being drawn at random out of a large ball.
    a. diverse
    b. arbitrary
    c. deliberate
    d. ubiquitous

30. Which of the following sentences is correct?
    a. I am going to buy a new car it is a blue sedan.
    b. I am going to buy a new car, it is a blue sedan.
    c. I am going to buy a new car; it is a blue sedan.
    d. I am going to buy a new car, therefore, it is a blue sedan.

Answers and Explanations

Mathematics

1. B: Begin by factoring the numerator. Assume that $x + 2$ (the denominator) is one of the factors for a quick start to the process. At this point, you should have the following: $2x^2 + x - 6 = (x + 2)(2x - ?)$. The first term of the second set of parentheses must be $2x$ because $2x^2 \div x = 2x$. The sign of the second set must be negative because a positive times a negative equals a negative, and the original problem has -6 as the final term in the numerator. To determine what replaces the "?" above, determine what number multiplied by 2 equals 6. The answer is 3. Now you have fully factored the numerator: $2x^2 + x - 6 = (x + 2)(2x - 3)$. Rewrite the original problem, substituting the factored numerator for the original numerator and solve: $\frac{2x^2 + x - 6}{x + 2} = \frac{(x + 2)(2x - 3)}{x + 2} = 2x - 3$

2. A: Begin by looking for anything that is common to all three terms. You should notice that each of the coefficients is divisible by three and that each of the x-terms has a power of 2 or more. Factor out a 3 from each term and you have $3(4x^4 - 9x^3 + 2x^2)$. Next, factor out x^2 from each term and you are left with $3x^2(4x^2 - 9x + 2)$. The portion inside the parentheses can be further factored as follows: $3x^2(4x^2 - 9x + 2) = 3x^2(4x - 1)(x - 2)$. This step may take a bit of trial and error, but you should be able to find it without too much trouble. Look at the answer choices to get a hint. If a combination you are considering is not a choice, then it is not the correct answer.

If you are having trouble factoring the problem, you can always work backwards. Look at the answer choices and multiply them out to see which one gives the original problem as its answer. This method is more time consuming, but it will yield a correct answer if you get stumped.

3. C: When you have two points (x_1, y_1) and (x_2, y_2), the formula for finding the distance d between them is $d = \sqrt{(x_2 - x_1)^2 + (y_2 - y_1)^2}$. Let $(x_1, y_1) = (-3, 4)$ and $(x_2, y_2) = (1, 6)$. Substituting these values into the formula gives $d = \sqrt{(1 + 3)^2 + (6 - 4)^2}$. Follow the proper order of operations: parentheses first, followed by exponents. $d = \sqrt{4^2 + 2^2} \rightarrow d = \sqrt{16 + 4} \rightarrow d = \sqrt{20}$. Do not leave your answer in this form. Always check to make sure you have reduced your answer as much as possible. Rewrite 20 as the product of a perfect square and another number:
$$d = \sqrt{20} \rightarrow d = \sqrt{4 \times 5} \rightarrow d = 2\sqrt{5}$$
If you have trouble remembering the distance formula, draw a quick graph of the two points and connect the dots. Treat that line as the hypotenuse of a right triangle and draw the other two sides. You can now tell the length of the other two sides, and then use the Pythagorean formula to get the length of the hypotenuse.

4. C: $(3x^{-2})^3 = 3^3 \times (x^{-2})^3 = 27 \times \left(\frac{1}{x^2}\right)^3 = 27x^{-6}$

5. A: Explanation: Since the second line, y=3, is a vertical, the intersection must occur at a point where $y = 3$. If $x = -1.5$, the equation describing the line is satisfied: $2(-1.5) + 3 = 0$.

6. A: From the starting expression, compute: $3\left(\frac{6x-3}{3}\right) - 3(9x+9)$= 3(2x-1)-27x-27= 6x-3-27x-27= -21x-30= 3(7x-10).

7. B: Compute as follows:$\left(3 - 2(2)\right)^2 = (3 - 4)^2 = -1^2 = 1.$

8. C: Rearranging the equation gives
3(y+4)=15(y-5), which is equivalent to
15y-3y=12+75, or
12y=87, and solving for y, $y = \frac{87}{12} = \frac{29}{4}$

9. B: The easiest pair to test is the third: $y = 4$ and $x = 0$. Substitute these values in each of the given equations and evaluate. Choice B gives 4 = 0 + 4, which is a true statement. None of the other answer choices is correct this number set.

10. D: The minus symbol in front of the parentheses can first be distributed, giving: $3x + 5y - 2y + 7x$, which reduces to $10x + 3y$.

11. C: The sum of the polynomials can be written as: $5x^2 - 4x + 1 - 3x^2 + x - 3$, which reduces to $2x^2 - 3x - 2$.

12. D: The polynomial can be factored as $(x - 7)(x + 3)$. Thus, $(x - 7)$ is a factor of the given polynomial.

13. B: The product given for Choice B can be written as $27x^3 - 9x^2y + 3xy^2 + 9x^2y - 3xy^2 + y^3$, which reduces to $27x^3 + y^3$.

14. C: The expression can be written as $(x - 3)(x - 3)$. Distribution gives $x^2 - 3x - 3x + 9$. Combining like terms gives $x^2 - 6x + 9$.

15. C: The zeros of an expression are the points at which the corresponding y-values are 0. Thus, the zeros of the expression, represented by the given factors, will occur at the x-values that have corresponding y-values of 0. Setting each factor equal to 0 gives $x + 6 = 0$ and $x - 7 = 0$. Solving for x gives $x = -6$ and $x = 7$. Thus, the zeros of the expression are $x = -6$ and $x = 7$.

16. C: Distributing each term in the expression, $x- 8$, across each term in the trinomial, gives $4x^4 - 2x^2 + 4x - 32x^3 + 16x - 32$. Writing the expression in standard form gives $4x^4 - 32x^3 - 2x^2 + 20x - 32$.

17. A: After distributing the minus sign across the second trinomial, the expression can be rewritten as $3x^3 - 9x^2 + 6x - 8x^3 - 4x^2 + 3x$. Combining like terms gives $-5x^3 - 13x^2 + 9x$.

18. D: The coefficients of the expanded polynomial are given by the fifth row of Pascal's triangle. Therefore, the coefficients are 1, 4, 6, 4, and 1, resulting in an expanded form of $a^4 + 4a^3b + 6a^2b^2 + 4ab^3 + b^4$. The expanded form may also be determined by using and evaluating combinations of 4 taken 0, 1, 2, 3, and 4 at a time. In other words, the expanded form may first be written as $\binom{4}{0} a^4b^0 + \binom{4}{1} a^3b^1 + \binom{4}{2} a^2b^2 + \binom{4}{3} a^1b^3 + \binom{4}{4} a^0b^4$. Notice each successive term shows a decrease on the power of a and an increase on the power of b. Also, the sum of the exponents for each term is 4. Since 4 combinations taken 0 at a time is 1, 4 combinations taken 1 at

a time is 4, and 4 combinations taken 2 at a time is 6, the expanded form may be written as shown above.

19. D: The denominator of the second rational expression may be factored as $(x + 8)(x + 2)$. Thus, the least common denominator of the two rational expressions is $(x + 8)(x + 2)$. Multiplying the top and bottom of the first fraction by $(x + 8)$, we see that $\frac{3}{x+2} = \frac{3(x+8)}{(x+2)(x+8)}$. The sum may be written as $\frac{3(x+8)+x}{(x+8)(x+2)}$, which simplifies to $\frac{4x+24}{(x+8)(x+2)}$. Factoring out a 4 in the numerator gives: $\frac{4(x+6)}{(x+8)(x+2)}$.

20. D: Multiplying each rational expression by the least common denominator of $2(x - 6)$. This procedure can be written as $\frac{x}{x-6} \cdot 2(x - 6) + \frac{1}{2} \cdot 2(x - 6) = \frac{6}{x-6} \cdot 2(x - 6)$. This simplifies to $2x + x - 6 = 12$. Solving for x gives $x = 6$. Substitution of this x-value into the original equation shows division by 0 in the rational expressions, $\frac{x}{x-6}$ and $\frac{6}{x-6}$. Therefore, 6 is an extraneous solution. There is no solution to the rational equation.

21. A: The expression represents the sum of two cubes; $a^3 + b^3 = (a + b)(a^2 - ab + b^2)$. Thus, $(2^3 + 4^3)$ can be written as $(2 + 4)(2^2 - (2)(4) + 4^2)$.

22. D: When the factors, $(x - 4)$ and $(x + 7)$ are multiplied, the x-terms sum to $3x$ and the constants produce a product of -28.

23. B: To find the midpoint between two complex numbers, add the complex numbers and divide by 2: $\frac{(-30+15i)+(12-3i)}{2} = \frac{-18+12i}{2} = -9 + 6i$.

24. C: Distances on the complex plane are calculated very much like they are on the real plane. To find the distance, use the distance formula $D = \sqrt{(x_1 - x_2)^2 + (y_1 - y_2)^2}$ with $a = x$ and $b = y$:
$$D = \sqrt{((-30) - 12)^2 + (15 - (-3))^2} = \sqrt{(-42)^2 + 18^2} \approx 46$$

25. C: It is quickest to find 30% of each answer given. (A:): 10% of 90 is 9, so 30% is 27. (B:): 10% of 180 is 18, so 30% is 54. (C:): 10% of 200 is 20, so 30% is 60. (D:): 10% of 210 is 21, so 30% is 63.

26. C: To solve, change the percent to a decimal: $0.40x = 18$
$$x = \frac{18}{0.40} = \frac{1800}{40} = 45$$

27. C: The difference 27 – 23 = 4, and 300% of 4 is 3 times 4, or 12.

28. D: To simplify the polynomial, group and combine all terms of the same order.
$$4x^3 + x - x^3 + 2x^2 + 3 - 3x^3 + x - 2x^2 - 1$$
$$= (4x^3 - x^3 - 3x^3) + (2x^2 - 2x^2) + (x + x) + (3 - 1)$$
$$= 0 + 0 + 2x + 2$$
$$= 2(x + 1)$$

29. B: The slope of a line is the change in y divided by the change in x. Calculate the slope as follows:
$$m = \frac{y_2 - y_1}{x_2 - x_1} = \frac{20 - 10}{6 - 1} = \frac{10}{5} = 2$$

30. C: The equation describes a functional relationship between y and $p(y)$. To solve the equation, substitute 4 as the value of y, such that $p(4) = \frac{4(4)}{2} + 5 = \frac{16}{2} + 5 = 8 + 5 = 13$.

Reading

1. B: This question basically asks for the main idea of the passage as a whole. Choice A is inappropriate because the passage does not discuss automotive stock. Choice B is a good choice because the final sentence of the first paragraph says exactly the same thing. Choice C is not only inappropriate, it is also only true for a very limited number of vehicles. Choice D is so general that it does not really say anything at all. The best choice is, therefore, Choice B.

2. B: Even if the meaning of "detriments" is unclear, the sentence it is used in provides some clues: "While there are many pros and cons associated with automobile ownership, many consumers do not adequately research the specifics benefits and <u>detriments</u> associated with purchasing a particular vehicle." The sentence's structure makes it probable that there is an identification of "pros and cons" with "benefits and detriments." Leaving this aside, if it clear that "pros" and "benefits" are the same thing, then it is likely that "cons" and "detriments" are the same thing. The best answer, then, is B, "Cons."

3. D: This is a detail question with tricky wording in the answer choices. The use of the term "always" should make the reader suspicious. In the real world, things are almost never "always" x or y. For example, choices A and D are explicitly contradicted in the second paragraph. Choice B is doubly inappropriate because of its use of "always" and its irrelevance to the passage (SUVs are not discussed in the passage). While choice C does not use "always," it is not a good choice because the relationship between color and cost is not discussed in the passage. Choice D is supported by the second paragraph and is the best overall choice.

4. D: Insofar as this is an "all of the above question," if the reader can confirm two of the answer choices, he or she need not examine the third. Choice A is a good one because the second paragraph says that the cost of a vehicle is not limited to purchase price alone. Choices B, C, and D are all included in the passage as additional costs of ownership, so since A has already been confirmed, confirming either B or C means that the correct answer is D.

5. B: According to the passage, choice A is inappropriate because if the consumer has done research, he or she will be less likely to be swayed by ancillary concerns. Choice B is explicitly stated in the final paragraph. Choice C is inappropriate because the passage says nothing about the consumer's attitude towards salespeople. Choice D is directly contradicted in the third paragraph. Thus, choice B is the best answer.

6. D: This is a difficult question because it is easy to make a simple mistake. The passage explicitly says that choices A and C can be explored on a manufacturer's website. While it seems likely that one could visit a manufacturer's website and find information on a vehicle's color, two things should be noted. First, the passage does not discuss a vehicle's color with reference to a manufacturer's website. Second, the passage does not discuss the

relationship between a vehicle's color and its cost. For both of these reasons, choice B is a poor choice; thus, the best answer is choice D.

7. D: Although the passage implies that Bill had not been in school for twenty years, the passage does not say how old Bill is. It might be tempting to try to extrapolate Bill's age from the passage, but this is impossible; in other words, Bill could be forty, fifty, or seventy-five years old (he must be older than twenty because he has not been at school for twenty years), but the passage gives no indication of exactly how old he is. Accordingly, D is the best answer.

8. D: In Bill's exchange with the girl-in-black, the passage shows that Bill is confused. It is also clear that Bill is sad—he misses Martha. The best answer, then, should mention Bill's confusion, his sadness, or both. Choice A mentions neither—this choice says that Bill is bored, or does not care about what is going on. Although Bill is somewhat reflective in the passage, B is not the best choice because it does not capture Bill's general state of mind. Choice C is not appropriate because even though Bill gets offended, he does not really get angry. Choice D is the best answer because it is directly supported by the passage: Bill cannot find the Biology labs, and he cannot understand why the cheerleaders do not thank him for holding the door open.

9. C: Like the first question in this section, it is tempting to tell a story to answer this question. The only information that is provided about Martha in the passage is that she is no longer with Bill. Since the passage says nothing about Martha's infidelity to Bill, choice A is unacceptable. Likewise, choice B may be eliminated because the passage remains noncommittal as to Martha's death. Choice C is a good choice because it succinctly describes Martha's relationship with Bill: she is somehow absent. Choice D is not supported by the passage. The best choice is C.

10. A: From the structure of the sentence, it is clear that "dumbfounded" means "could not understand." Choice A is a good choice because "perplexed" is a synonym of confused. Choice B is inappropriate because if something is "rationalized," it is explained or justified. Choice C is inappropriate because "dilapidated" means run-down. To "entreat" means to beg or ask for something; thus, choice D is inappropriate. To "perseverate" means to obsessively focus on something, and while some might think that Bill focuses on rudeness more than is necessary. Thus, A is the best choice.

11. C: The passage says nothing about Bill's past profession, so any inferences drawn about his work are in error. Choices A and B are therefore unacceptable. C is a good choice because the final paragraph has a sense of finality about it—Bill is leaving the school, and it is unlikely that he will return. Choice D is not supported by the passage. If Bill misses Martha as much as he says, then it is likely that he really does love her. The best answer is choice C.

12. C: From the sentences preceding the sentence where "diminution" occurs, the reader knows "diminution" must refer to "a process whereby a given liquid is slowly simmered until its volume diminishes." "Diminution" must mean something like "lessening." Choice A is inappropriate because "process" is too general. Choice B is inappropriate because "liquid" would be redundant in the sentence. Choice C captures the idea of "lessening." Although one could make a case for choice D, choice C is the best fit with the sentence.

13. D: This question is tricky because a number of the answer choices seem correct but are not supported by the passage. Choice A seems reasonable, but the passage does not say anything about how performing reductions demonstrates skill. Choices B and C also seem reasonable—if reductions are in many dishes, then restaurant customers probably like them, which means that they are popular in contemporary cuisine. However, the passage does not say these things. The passage does explicitly say that many recipes call for reductions, so choice D is a good answer. Therefore, D is the best answer.

14. B: This question asks for a specific detail from the passage. Rereading the relevant portion of the passage is thus a wise strategy. Rereading the passage reveals that the chicken is browned and removed, then the butter is added followed by the wine. Turning to the answers, it is obvious that B is the best choice.

15. D: According to the passage, the wine and butter mixture should be reduced by half. After this, chicken stock and chicken breasts should be added. The sauce in this new mixture should be reduced by half. This results in two reductions (A and C in the answer choices). Choice B is not a reduction, according to the passage. The best answer choice is D because it includes the two reductions without mentioning the butter.

16. C: This question initially seems straightforward, but it can be misleading. When the choices are considered individually, it becomes clear that choice A is inappropriate because it contradicts the passage. A common mistake is over boiling, not under boiling. Choice B is likewise contradicted by the passage. Adding butter is part of the chicken Marsala recipe. Since two of the choices have thus far been eliminated, choice D can be eliminated. Choice C is a good answer because the passage describes how adding starches can diminish a sauce's flavor and make it too thick.

17. B: Without looking at the answer choices, a reader may answer this question along the following lines: "the chicken Marsala recipe is an example of a reduction." Choice A seems right, but the importance of reductions is really demonstrated by the first paragraph: reductions are important because they are present in many recipes. Choice B is a close match to "the chicken Marsala recipe is an example of a reduction," and so it is a good preliminary choice. Choice C is inappropriate because it is unclear what a demonstration of "how not to do a reduction" would consist of. Choice D is obviously incorrect. The reader's experience is not discussed in the passage. The best answer is therefore B.

18. A: This question asks for a detail from the passage. According to the passage, Choice A is the only answer choice that is true—in the third paragraph it explicitly says that grieving individuals can be self-destructive. Choice B is not appropriate because the passage does not mention therapy. Choice C is not appropriate because the passage does not discuss complete, or full, healing; it says that the bereaved can begin to heal when they move beyond anger. Choice D is not appropriate because the passage does not mention crying.

19. D: This question is difficult because the first paragraph of the passage is largely introductory. While the paragraph seems to be concerned with the different stages of the grieving process, these stages serve as context for the main idea of the paragraph: the anger stage of the grieving process is both natural and misunderstood. Choice D is the best choice. Choice A is not discussed in the passage. Choice B is partially contradicted by the first paragraph. Choice C is a detail from paragraph three.

20. D: Even if the one does not know the meaning of "cathartic," closely examining the sentence's structure can help determine what the word means. The "in other words" sentence construction alerts the reader that what follows is a restatement of what comes before; thus, "cathartic" and "therapeutic" are related to the phrase "emotional release and allows for the beginning of the healing process." Since something "therapeutic" clearly "allows for the beginning of the healing process," it stands to reason that something "cathartic" is related to "emotional release," which is exactly what answer choice D says.

21. B: Although this question seems to ask for a detail, it actually asks for a larger point from the passage. Choice B is the only good choice because paragraph three discusses how individuals can come to understand how tragedy is generally blameless. Choices A, C, and D, are all inappropriate because the passage does not address them.

22. D: This question asks for a detail from the passage. Choice A is not a good answer because it is directly contradicted by the passage—anger helps with the grieving process. Choices B and C, while probably true, are not discussed in the passage and so are inappropriate answers. The only remaining choice is D, which is explicitly stated in the fourth paragraph of the passage.

23. D: This question is similar to the previous question. It is a detail question that lists "all of the above" as a possible answer choice. The passage tells the reader that people who fail to go through the grieving process may experience vague, continued irritability, so answer choice A seems good. Choice B also looks good because the fourth paragraph explicitly states that such individuals may lose religious faith. Because two answer choices are obviously correct, choice C does not even have to be examined—the correct answer choice must be D, all of the above.

24. D: The passage describes the artistry of Greek coinage and gives the reasons why so much effort went into designing them.

25. A: "Delectation" means to savor or to enjoy the flavor or beauty of something, in this case the design of the coins.

26. D: The word is defined in passing in the text in the second sentence.

27. D: The sentence contrasts the artistic content of the coins with their use as a practical means of commercial exchange

28. B: The frequent need for new designs meant that the artisans who did the work had ample opportunity to perfect their skills.

29. D: The passage describes the coins as artistic objects, not simply because they were the first coins, but also because of the historical situation which is described, and which led to their being designed with great care and pride.

30. B: The first sentence shows that the author thinks of coins as utilitarian objects and that few of them are designed in a manner that makes them worth considering as something more than that.

Writing

1. A: because a comma should follow a state name when it is used in this format. When a state name follows a city name, it become a non-essential clause and should be set off by commas. Choice B is incorrect because *it's* is a contraction for *it is* while *its* (without the apostrophe) is the possessive form of the word *it.* Choice C is incorrect because *buildings and places* is a two-item series connected by *and*; a comma should not be used in a two-item series written in this format. Choice D is incorrect for the same reason; the phrase is a two-item series connected by *and*.

2. B: is the correct answer because *Back in 1634* is a non-essential clause beginning the sentence and should be separated from the rest of the sentence by a comma. Choice A is incorrect because years should be written using Arabic numerals; they should not be written out. Choice C is incorrect for the opposite reason; in an essay, ordinals should be written out rather than using Arabic numerals. Choice D is incorrect because *unusually* changes the meaning of the sentence. Using the word *usually* helps indicate that the Boston Common was most often used for livestock but also had other uses.

3. D: because this choice most effectively explains how the New State House got its name. Choice A is incorrect because the word order of the sentence makes it difficult to understand why the New State House got its name; the dependent clause is not adequately supported. Choice B is incorrect because it changes the meaning of the sentence; the new building got its name from the old, not the other way around. Choice C is incorrect because it is in the passive voice and wordier from the correct answer.

4. A: because the correct spelling of the word *cemetery* ends with an –ery. Choice B is incorrect because a comma should only be used before a conjunction if the conjunction precedes an independent clause. Choice C is incorrect because *its* without an apostrophe is the possessive form of *it.* Choice D is incorrect because *grain storage* is not a series or list, which means the words should not be separated by a comma.

5. D: because this version of the sentence is the most succinct and clear. Choice A is incorrect because the sentence is in the passive voice. Choice B is incorrect because it is not as clearly worded as choice D. Choice B separates the list of people from the reason why they are important (they are some of the most famous people in the cemetery), which makes the sentence difficult to understand. Choice C is incorrect because it is missing a comma after *Massacre* and because the sentence doesn't qualify how famous the people are. Only choice D explains that the people listed are the most famous people buried at the Granary.

6. A: Using the male-pronoun, such as "his," once was proper when referring to an unspecified person. However, this practice is now considered gender biased, as it does not take the possibility that the person could be female into account. Today the best way to indicate an unspecified person is with pronoun phrases that take both genders into account, such "his or her," "he or she," or "him or her."

7. C: In the context of this sentence, the word redundant should appear in its noun form, which is redundancy (meaning "unnecessary repetition"). Redundant is an adjective, and redundantly is an adverb. Redundance may sound like a proper word, but it is not.

8. D: Although the serial comma, which is the comma that immediately precedes a coordinating conjunction ("and"), is contested, its use is perfectly proper according to such reliable sources as the Chicago Manual of Style. However, randomly inserted commas are improper, which is why choices B and D are incorrect. Choice A misses the essential hyphen that should join the adjective phrase "cross-country."

9. A: Condolence is an expression of sympathy, and only choice A spells it correctly.

10. D: Although the word inquisition means a prolonged process of questioning, it is not spelled with an <e>, as is question. The correct spelling uses an <i>, as in inquire.

11. A: Adjective phrases consisting of more than one word (compound modifiers) should be hyphenated, even if the person, place, or thing they're describing is only implied. The word child is only implied in this sentence, but the adjective phrase describing it—"two-year-old"—still needs to be fully hyphenated in order for it to be correct.

12. C: "Read" (present tense form of the verb) maintains the parallel structure of the sentence and matches the verb tense for "revise" and "complete." The other answer choices represent the present participle ("reading"), infinitive ("to read"), and future tense ("will read") of the word.

13. A: The correct spelling of the word is "indigenous."

14. B: The word "docile" means easily taught or ready to be taught. The sentence should read: Peter is so talented with horses that the skittish colt became docile once Peter took over his training.

15. D: The sentence should read: King George III was determined to have the American colonists pay taxes to Britain on items such as tea and paper.

16. B: The sentence should read: Susan B. Anthony was outraged that women were denied the same rights as men, such as equal pay and the right to vote.

17. C: The context of the sentence and use of the phrase "quickly moving on" indicate that the immigration officer is in a hurry and does not spend a lot of time examining Maria's passport.

18. B: "Representative" acts as a noun and "represent" as a verb. The sentence should read: As a student council representative, Travis endeavored to represent his peers to the best of his ability.

19. C: Personification is an expression in which animals or objects are attributed with human characteristics. In the given sentence, the trees are attributed with the human ability to wave a fond farewell.

20. C: The sentence should read: Harper Lee wrote *To Kill a Mockingbird* as an exposé of social injustice.

21. A: The syntax of this sentence is correct. It uses a comma to offset the subordinate clause ("Because she wanted to reduce unnecessary waste") from the independent clause ("Cicily decided to have the television repaired instead of buying a new one"). Placing the independent clause, which is the most important idea in the sentence, at the end for emphasis also makes the sentence stronger.

22. B: The sentence compares the melody of a pop song to that of the first movement in Beethoven's ninth symphony. Therefore, concluding that they probably are similar is logical. The pop song reminds the speaker of the Beethoven piece, which means the pop song suggests the melody of the Beethoven piece. Reminiscent and suggestive are synonyms in this context.

23. B: That Julie may have to study on the day she and the speaker consider going to the park means their plans are uncertain. The plans might happen, but they also might not happen. Based on this context, you can conclude that the word tentative means "uncertain." Because the speaker does not indicate that either the plan to go to the park or the possibility Julie may have to study is more likely, unlikely is not the best answer choice.

24. C: According to the sentence, while certain things could not be seen through the curtains, light could. As a result, the curtains are not transparent enough to see the street, yet they are transparent enough to see sunshine. The prefix "semi" means "partially." Based on this context, you can conclude that translucent and semi-transparent share the same meaning. Although something that is flimsy may be transparent, this is not always the case, so the words are not synonyms. Transitory shares the root word "trans," meaning "through," but it means "not lasting." Something that is opaque does not allow light to pass through it, which is the opposite of translucent.

25. B: Contempt is a feeling of scorn or disdain, and to be contemptuous is to express that feeling. Contemptible is something that inspired contempt, which in Veronica's case, would be the noisy construction workers. Contemptful is not a real word.

26. C: A word's origin, or etymology, will give you a clue to its meaning. A brass ring merely gilded with gold, a fawney, is hardly the same thing as a solid gold ring. Attempting to pass of such a ring as pure gold would be untruthful and the ring would only be a fake gold ring. The words phony and fake share the same meaning. Although fawning sounds and looks similar to fawney, the former means flattering or submissive, which provides no indication of the real meaning of fawney.

27. B: The correct spelling of the word is "deleterious."

28. D: It is appropriate to use a colon to introduce a list. It is not appropriate to use a colon following a preposition (choice B) or after the phrases "including" and "for example," which make the use of a colon redundant (choices A and C).

29. B: The word "arbitrary" means random or determined by chance. The sentence should read: The selection of the winning lottery numbers is entirely arbitrary with numbers being drawn at random out of a large ball.

30. C: "I am going to buy a new car" and "it is a blue sedan" are independent clauses (they each contain a subject and a verb and express a complete thought). It is appropriate to join two independent clauses in a single sentence with a semicolon. Choice A is a run-on sentence. Choice B is a comma splice. Choice D uses a comma to precede the conjunctive adverb "therefore," which is incorrect.

Practice Test #2

Practice Questions

Mathematics

1. Which of the following represents the factors of the expression, $x^2 - 3x - 40$?
    a. $(x - 8)(x + 5)$
    b. $(x - 7)(x + 4)$
    c. $(x + 10)(x - 4)$
    d. $(x + 6)(x - 9)$

2. Which of the following expressions is equivalent to the expression, $\frac{x-4}{x^2+4x-32}$?
    a. $\frac{x-4}{x+8}$
    b. $\frac{x-4}{(x+4)(x+8)}$
    c. $\frac{1}{x+8}$
    d. $x + 8$

3. Which of the following expressions is equivalent to the expression, $\frac{x-3}{x^3-6x^2-9x+54}$?
    a. $\frac{x-3}{x-6}$
    b. $\frac{1}{(x+3)(x-6)}$
    c. $\frac{1}{x-6}$
    d. $\frac{x-3}{(x+3)(x-6)}$

4. Given the equation, $2^x = 64$, what is the value of x?
    a. 4
    b. 5
    c. 6
    d. 7

5. Given the equation, $\frac{2}{x+4} = \frac{3}{x}$, what is the value of x?
    a. 10
    b. 12
    c. -12
    d. -14

6. What are the factors of the following polynomial: $2x^2 + 7x - 15$?
    a. $(2x + 5)(x - 3)$
    b. $(x + 5)(2x - 3)$
    c. $(2x - 5)(x + 3)$
    d. $(x - 5)(2x + 3)$

7. What is the solution to the following equation: $x^2 - 9 = 0$?

    a. $x = 3$

    b. $x = -3$

    c. Both A and B are solutions to the equation

    d. Neither A nor B is a solution to the equation

8. Line Q has a slope of 10 and intercepts the y axis at point (0, -15). What is the equation of line Q?

    a. $y = -15$

    b. $y = -15x + 10$

    c. $y = 15x - 10$

    d. $y = 10x - 15$

9. The equation for line 1 is $y_x = 2x_1 + 6$ and the equation for line 2 is $y_2 = -x_2 - 3$. At what point does line 1 intersect line 2?

    a. (-3, 6)

    b. (6, -3)

    c. (-3, 0)

    d. (0,-3)

10. Joshua has to earn more than 92 points on the state test in order to qualify for an academic scholarship. Each question is worth 4 points, and the test has a total of 30 questions. Let x represent the number of test questions.

Which of the following graphs best represents the number of questions Joshua must answer correctly?

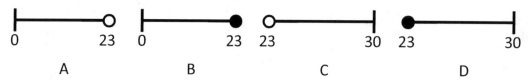

    A   B   C   D

    a. Graph A

    b. Graph B

    c. Graph C

    d. Graph D

11. Simplify the expression $x^5 \cdot (2x)^3$.

    a. $2x^8$

    b. $2x^{15}$

    c. $8x^8$

    d. $8x^{15}$

12. Solve the equation $3x^2 + 4x = 8$ for x.

    a. $-\frac{2}{3} \pm \frac{2}{3}\sqrt{7}$

    b. $-\frac{8}{3} \pm \frac{2}{3}\sqrt{7}$

    c. $-4 \pm 4\sqrt{7}$

    d. $4 \pm \frac{2}{3}\sqrt{7}$

13. Simplify the expression $\frac{x^2+2x-24}{5x-20}$.

    a. $\frac{x-4}{5}$

    b. $\frac{x+6}{5}$

    c. $\frac{(x-4)(x+6)}{5(x-4)}$

    d. $\frac{(x+4)(x+6)}{5(x-4)}$

14. Simplify the expression $x^6 \cdot (3x)^2$.

    a. $3x^8$

    b. $3x^{12}$

    c. $9x^8$

    d. $9x^{12}$

15. Solve the equation $x^2 + 4x + 8 = 0$ for x.

    a. $x = -4$ and $x = 0$

    b. $x = 0$ and $x = 4$

    c. $x = -2 \pm 2i$

    d. $x = 2 \pm 2i$

16. Solve the equation $3x^2 - 3x + 7 = 0$ for x.

    a. $x = -\frac{1}{2} \pm \frac{5i}{6}\sqrt{3}$

    b. $x = \frac{1}{2} \pm \frac{5i}{6}\sqrt{3}$

    c. $x = -1 \pm 5i\sqrt{3}$

    d. $x = 1 \pm 5i\sqrt{3}$

17. Solve the equation $\frac{5}{x} - \frac{6}{x+2} = 1$ for x.

    a. $x = -2$

    b. $x = 2$

    c. $x = -5$ and $x = -2$

    d. $x = -5$ and $x = 2$

18. Solve the equation $\frac{x^2+5x-6}{x^2-1} = 2$ for x.

    a. $x = -4$

    b. $x = 4$

    c. $x = 6$

    d. $x = 7$

19. What percent of the grid is shaded? (Assume all small squares are the same size)

    a. 52.5%
    b. 60%
    c. 62.5%
    d. 70%

20. 30% of _____ = 18
    a. 54
    b. 60
    c. 66
    d. 75

21. Evaluate $x^2 - (2y - 3)$ if $x = 4$ and $y = 3$.
    a. 12
    b. 13
    c. 10
    d. 8

22. For all nonzero values of q, r, and s, the expression $-\dfrac{12q^3r^4s^3}{3r^2s^4}$ is equivalent to:
    a. $4\dfrac{qr^2s}{s^2}$
    b. $-4qrs$
    c. $-4\dfrac{q^3r^2}{s}$
    d. $4qrs$

23. What is the slope of the line described by the equation $= 17x - 4$?
    a. 17
    b. -17
    c. 4
    d. -4

24. Solve the equation $2x^2 - 2x + 14 = 0$ for x.
    a. $x = -\dfrac{1}{2} \pm \dfrac{3i}{2}\sqrt{3}$
    b. $x = \dfrac{1}{2} \pm \dfrac{3i}{2}\sqrt{3}$
    c. $x = -1 \pm 3i\sqrt{3}$
    d. $x = 1 \pm 3i\sqrt{3}$

25. What is the value of the y-intercept of the line described by the equation $2x + 3y - 7 = 0$?
    a. 7
    b. -7
    c. $\dfrac{7}{3}$
    d. $-\dfrac{7}{3}$

26. Simplify the expression $\frac{x^2-3x-18}{5x-30}$.

   a. $\frac{x-6}{5}$

   b. $\frac{x+3}{5}$

   c. $\frac{(x-3)(x+6)}{5(x-6)}$

   d. $\frac{(x+3)(x+6)}{5(x-6)}$

27. Simplify the expression $x^5 \cdot (2x)^3$.

   a. $2x^8$

   b. $2x^{15}$

   c. $8x^8$

   d. $8x^{15}$

28. Solve the equation $x^2 + 2x + 10 = 0$ for x.

   a. $x = -4$ and $x = 2$

   b. $x = -2$ and $x = 4$

   c. $x = -1 \pm 3i$

   d. $x = 1 \pm 3i$

29. What are the factors of the following polynomial: $x^2 - x - 56$?

   a. $(x - 7)(x + 8)$

   b. $(x + 7)(x - 8)$

   c. $(x - 7)(x - 8)$

   d. $(x + 7)(x + 8)$

30. What is the simplest form of the following polynomial:
$$4x^3 + 5x - x^3 + 2x^2 + 17 - 3x^3 + 5x - 2x^2 + 3$$

   a. $10x + 20$

   b. $x + 2$

   c. $10(x + 2)$

   d. $x^3 + 2$

Reading

Reading:

Read each passage carefully. Since the assessment is not timed, take as much time as you need to read each passage. Each passage may have one or more questions.

A helpful strategy is to focus on the opening and ending sentences of each paragraph to identify the main idea. Another strategy is to look for key words or phrases within the passage that indicate the author's purpose or the meaning.

Reading Sample Questions:

Read the passage below and answer questions 1-5.

Chang-Rae Lee's debut and award-winning novel <u>Native Speaker</u> is about Henry Park, a Korean-American individual who struggles to find his place as an immigrant in a suburb of New York City. This novel addresses the notion that as the individuals who know us best, our family, peers, and lovers are the individuals who direct our lives and end up defining us. Henry Park is confronted with this reality in the very beginning of the novel, which begins:

The day my wife left she gave me a list of who I was.

Upon separating from his wife, Park struggles with racial and ethnic identity issues due to his loneliness. Through Parks' work as an undercover operative for a private intelligence agency, the author presents the theme of espionage as metaphor for the internal divide that Park experiences as an immigrant. This dual reality creates two worlds for Park and increases his sense of uncertainty with regard to his place in society. While he constantly feels like an outsider looking in, he also feels like he belongs to neither world.

Chang-Rae Lee is also a first-generation Korean American immigrant. He immigrated to America at the early age of three. Themes of identity, race, and cultural alienation pervade his works. His interests in these themes no doubt stem from his first-hand experience as a kid growing up in a Korean household while going to an American school. Lee is also author of <u>A Gesture Life</u> and <u>Aloft</u>. The protagonists are similar in that they deal with labels placed on them based on race, color, and language. Consequently, all of these characters struggle to belong in America.

Lee's novels address differences within a nation's mix of race, religion, and history, and the necessity of assimilation between cultures. In his works and through his characters, Lee shows us both the difficulties and the subtleties of the immigrant experience in America. He urges us to consider the role of borders and to consider why the idea of opening up one's borders is so frightening. In an ever-changing world in which cultures are becoming more intermingled, the meaning of identity must be constantly redefined, especially when the security of belonging to a place is becoming increasingly elusive. As our world grows smaller with increasing technological advances, these themes in Lee's novels become even more pertinent.

1. Which of the following best describes the purpose of this passage?
   a. to criticize
   b. to analyze
   c. to entertain
   d. to inform

2. Why does the author of the passage quote the first line of the novel Native Speaker?
   a. to illustrate one of the themes in the novel
   b. to show how the book is semi-autobiographical
   c. it is the main idea of the novel
   d. to create interest in the novel

3. According to the passage, which of the following is not a main theme of Lee's novels?
   e. identity
   f. culture
   g. immigration
   h. espionage

4. Based on the passage, why do Lee's novels focus on race and cultural identity?
   a. because Lee was born in Korea
   b. because Lee's ancestors are Korean
   c. because Lee immigrated to America at a young age
   d. because Lee feels these issues are the biggest problem facing America

5. How does the author of the passage feel about the ideas presented in Lee's novels?
   a. concerned about the disappearance of cultures in a rapidly expanding and mixed world
   b. excited that immigrants are easily able to redefine and establish themselves in new cultures
   c. certain that all borders will eventually be eliminated so world cultures will commingle and fully assimilate
   d. critical regarding the role technology has played in society and how it destroys the immigrant experience

Questions 6-10 pertain to the following excerpt.

Excerpt from Emma
by Jane Austen

Emma Woodhouse, handsome, clever, and rich, with a comfortable home and happy disposition, seemed to unite some of the best blessings of existence; and had lived nearly twenty-one years in the world with very little to distress or <u>vex</u> her.

She was the youngest of the two daughters of a most affectionate, indulgent father; and had, in consequence of her sister's marriage, been mistress of his house from a very early period. Her mother had died too long ago for her to have more than an indistinct remembrance of her caresses; and her place had been supplied by an excellent woman as governess, who had fallen little short of a mother in affection. Sixteen years had Miss Taylor been in Mr. Woodhouse's family, less as a governess than a friend, very fond of both daughters, but particularly of Emma. Between them it was more the intimacy of sisters. Even before Miss Taylor had ceased to hold the nominal office of governess, the mildness of her temper had hardly allowed her to impose any restraint; and the shadow of authority being now long passed away, they had been living together as friend and friend very mutually attached, and Emma doing just what she liked; highly esteeming Miss Taylor's judgment, but directed chiefly by her own.

The real evils, indeed, of Emma's situation were the power of having rather too much her own way, and a disposition to think a little too well of herself; these were the disadvantages which threatened her many enjoyments. The danger, however, was at present so unperceived, that they did not by any means rank as misfortunes with her.

Sorrow came—a gentle sorrow—but not at all in the shape of any disagreeable consciousness—Miss Taylor married. It was Miss Taylor's loss which first brought grief. It was on the wedding-day of this beloved friend that Emma first sat in mournful thought of any continuance. The wedding over, and the bride-people gone, her father and herself were left to dine together, with no prospect of a third to cheer a long evening. Her father composed himself to sleep after dinner, as usual, and she had then only to sit and think of what she had lost.

The event had every promise of happiness for her friend. Mr. Weston was a man of unexceptionable character, easy fortune, suitable age, and pleasant manners; and there was some satisfaction in considering with what self-denying, generous friendship she had always wished and promoted the match; but it was a black morning's work for her. The want of Miss Taylor would be felt every hour of every day. She recalled her past kindness—the kindness, the affection of sixteen years— how she had taught and how she had played with her from five years old—how she had devoted all her powers to attach and amuse her in health—and how nursed her through the various illnesses of childhood. A large debt of gratitude was owing here...the equal footing and perfect unreserve which had soon followed Isabella's marriage, on their being left to each other, was yet a dearer, tenderer recollection. She had been a friend and companion such as few possessed: intelligent, well-informed, useful, gentle, knowing all the ways of the family, interested in all its concerns, and peculiarly interested in herself, in every pleasure, every scheme of hers—one to whom she could speak every thought as it arose, and who had such an affection for her as could never find fault.

How was she to bear the change?—It was true that her friend was going only half a mile from them; but Emma was aware that great must be the difference between a Mrs. Weston, only half a mile from them, and a Miss Taylor in the house; and with all her advantages, natural and domestic, she was now in great danger of suffering from intellectual solitude. She dearly loved her father, but he was no companion for her. He could not meet her in conversation, rational or playful.

The evil of the actual disparity in their ages (and Mr. Woodhouse had not married early) was much increased by his constitution and habits; for having been a valetudinarian all his life, without activity of mind or body, he was a much older man in ways than in years; and though everywhere beloved for the friendliness of his heart and his amiable temper, his talents could not have recommended him at any time.

Her sister, though comparatively but little removed by matrimony, being settled in London, only sixteen miles off, was much beyond her daily reach; and many a long October and November evening must be struggled through at Hartfield, before Christmas brought the next visit from Isabella and her husband, and their little children, to fill the house, and give her pleasant society again.

6. How does Miss Taylor's marriage affect Emma?
   a. Miss Taylor's marriage disrupts the comfort Emma had enjoyed all her life.
   b. Emma was happy her friend was marrying a wonderful man.
   c. Emma regards the change as a challenge and opportunity for intellectual growth.
   d. Miss Taylor's marriage makes Emma think about getting married herself.

7. As used in the first paragraph, what does the word vex mean?
   a. interest
   b. fulfill
   c. support
   d. displease

8. Based on this excerpt, Emma can be described as
   a. unfortunate.
   b. devious.
   c. selfish.
   d. studious.

9. How do themes of class and maturity interact in this excerpt?
   a. Emma's upper-class background gives her greater access to education, thereby making her more interested in intellectual stimulation than a less mature person might be.
   b. The privilege that comes with an upper-class background can prevent a person from having the necessary skills for dealing with change in a mature way.
   c. Emma's first twenty-one years were so happy because she enjoyed a privileged, upper-class lifestyle, and that happiness made her a more mature person.
   d. Having people constantly take care of her has prevented Emma from developing feelings of kindness and love for others.

10. Why does the author describe Miss Taylor's wedding as a "black morning's work"?
   a. Emma has to work to pretend she is happy about the wedding.
   b. The day of Miss Taylor's wedding is a bad day for Emma.
   c. Emma worked hard to organize the wedding.
   d. The wedding party dresses in black.

Questions 11-15 pertain to the following excerpt.
Excerpt from The Federalist No. 1
By Alexander Hamilton
To the People of the State of New York:
AFTER an unequivocal experience of the inefficacy of the subsisting federal government, you are called upon to deliberate on a new Constitution for the United States of America. The subject speaks its own importance; comprehending in its consequences nothing less than the existence of the UNION, the safety and welfare of the parts of which it is composed, the fate of an empire in many respects the most interesting in the world. It has been frequently remarked that it seems to have been reserved to the people of this country, by their conduct and example, to decide the important question, whether societies of men are really capable or not of establishing good government from reflection and choice, or whether they are forever destined to depend for their political constitutions on accident and force. If there be any truth in the remark, the crisis at which we are arrived may with propriety be regarded as the era in which that decision is to be made; and a wrong election of the part we shall act may, in this view, deserve to be considered as the general misfortune of mankind.
This idea will add the inducements of philanthropy to those of patriotism, to heighten the solicitude which all considerate and good men must feel for the event. Happy will it be if our choice should be directed by a judicious estimate of our true interests, unperplexed and unbiased by considerations not connected with the

public good. But this is a thing more ardently to be wished than seriously to be expected. The plan offered to our deliberations affects too many particular interests, innovates upon too many local institutions, not to involve in its discussion a variety of objects foreign to its merits, and of views, passions and prejudices little favorable to the discovery of truth.

Among the most formidable of the obstacles which the new Constitution will have to encounter may readily be distinguished the obvious interest of a certain class of men in every State to resist all changes which may hazard a diminution of the power, emolument, and consequence of the offices they hold under the State establishments; and the perverted ambition of another class of men, who will either hope to aggrandize themselves by the confusions of their country, or will flatter themselves with fairer prospects of elevation from the subdivision of the empire into several partial confederacies than from its union under one government.

It is not, however, my design to dwell upon observations of this nature. I am well aware that it would be disingenuous to resolve indiscriminately the opposition of any set of men (merely because their situations might subject them to suspicion) into interested or ambitious views. Candor will oblige us to admit that even such men may be actuated by upright intentions; and it cannot be doubted that much of the opposition which has made its appearance, or may hereafter make its appearance, will spring from sources, blameless at least, if not respectable—the honest errors of minds led astray by preconceived jealousies and fears. So numerous indeed and so powerful are the causes which serve to give a false bias to the judgment, that we, upon many occasions, see wise and good men on the wrong as well as on the right side of questions of the first magnitude to society. This circumstance, if duly attended to, would furnish a lesson of moderation to those who are ever so much persuaded of their being in the right in any controversy. And a further reason for caution, in this respect, might be drawn from the reflection that we are not always sure that those who advocate the truth are influenced by purer principles than their antagonists. Ambition, avarice, personal animosity, party opposition, and many other motives not more laudable than these, are apt to operate as well upon those who support as those who oppose the right side of a question. Were there not even these inducements to moderation, nothing could be more ill-judged than that intolerant spirit which has, at all times, characterized political parties. For in politics, as in religion, it is equally absurd to aim at making proselytes by fire and sword. Heresies in either can rarely be cured by persecution. And yet, however just these sentiments will be allowed to be, we have already sufficient indications that it will happen in this as in all former cases of great national discussion. A torrent of angry and malignant passions will be let loose. To judge from the conduct of the opposite parties, we shall be led to conclude that they will mutually hope to evince the justness of their opinions, and to increase the number of their converts by the loudness of their declamations and the bitterness of their invectives. An enlightened zeal for the energy and efficiency of government will be stigmatized as the offspring of a temper fond of despotic power and hostile to the principles of liberty. An over-scrupulous jealousy of danger to the rights of the people, which is more commonly the fault of the head than of the heart, will be represented as mere pretense and artifice, the stale bait for popularity at the expense of the public good. It will be forgotten, on the one hand, that jealousy is the usual concomitant of love, and that the noble enthusiasm of liberty is apt to be infected with a spirit of narrow and illiberal distrust. On the other hand, it will be equally forgotten that the vigor of government is essential to the security of liberty;

that, in the contemplation of a sound and well-informed judgment, their interest can never be separated; and that a dangerous ambition more often lurks behind the specious mask of zeal for the rights of the people than under the forbidden appearance of zeal for the firmness and efficiency of government. History will teach us that the former has been found a much more certain road to the introduction of despotism than the latter, and that of those men who have overturned the liberties of republics, the greatest number have begun their career by paying an <u>obsequious</u> court to the people; commencing demagogues, and ending tyrants.

11. How does the opening of this excerpt affect the writer's argument?
   a. By criticizing the United States Constitution explicitly, he is challenging readers to look at old institutions in new ways that may have positive effects on the federal government.
   b. By portraying the subsisting federal government as suffering from inefficacy, he is seeking to alienate overly patriotic readers.
   c. By saying that it is up to "the people of this country" to establish a "good government," he is suggesting that he expects input from his fellow Americans regarding how to improve the United States Constitution.
   d. By drawing attention to the "unequivocal inefficacy" of the subsisting federal government, Alexander Hamilton immediately explains why the federal government is in need of change.

12. What effect does the author's use of first-person point of view have on his argument?
   a. It attempts to establish agreement between the reader and himself.
   b. It establishes an informal tone that makes him seem friendlier and more approachable.
   c. It forces the reader to feel responsibility for the federal government's problems.
   d. It implies the reader also needs to suggest methods for improving the federal government.

13. Which of the following sentences from the excerpt exemplifies an attempt to sway the reader's opinion of the writer's opponents?
   a. And yet, however just these sentiments will be allowed to be, we have already sufficient indications that it will happen in this as in all former cases of great national discussion.
   b. For in politics, as in religion, it is equally absurd to aim at making proselytes by fire and sword.
   c. To judge from the conduct of the opposite parties, we shall be led to conclude that they will mutually hope to evince the justness of their opinions, and to increase the number of their converts by the loudness of their declamations and the bitterness of their invectives.
   d. This idea will add the inducements of philanthropy to those of patriotism, to heighten the solicitude which all considerate and good men must feel for the event.

14. Why does the writer follow paragraph 3 by stating, "It is not, however, my design to dwell upon observations of this nature"?
   a. He regrets criticizing politicians currently holding office and wants the reader to focus on the less inflammatory details in his argument.
   b. He wants to give the impression that the purpose of his argument is not to merely criticize politicians who are currently holding office.
   c. He realizes he lacks the information to continue criticizing politicians currently holding office and cannot continue his argument.
   d. He believes that criticizing politicians currently holding office is a weak way to present his argument and will stop doing so.

15. As used in the final sentence of the excerpt, what does the word obsequious mean?
   a. submissive
   b. free
   c. revolutionary
   d. dominant

Questions 16 – 23 pertain to the following story:

<u>Anna Karenina</u>

By Leo Tolstoy

The young Princess Kitty Shtcherbatskaya was eighteen. It was the first winter that she had been out in the world. Her success in society had been greater than that of either of her elder sisters, and greater even than her mother had anticipated. To say nothing of the young men who danced at the Moscow balls being almost all in love with Kitty, two serious suitors had already this first winter made their appearance: Levin, and immediately after his departure, Count Vronsky.

Levin's appearance at the beginning of the winter, his frequent visits, and evident love for Kitty, had led to the first serious conversations between Kitty's parents as to her future, and to disputes between them. The prince was on Levin's side; he said he wished for nothing better for Kitty. The princess for her part, going round the question in the manner peculiar to women, maintained that Kitty was too young, that Levin had done nothing to prove that he had serious intentions, that Kitty felt no great attraction to him, and other side issues; but she did not state the principal point, which was that she looked for a better match for her daughter, and that Levin was not to her liking, and she did not understand him. When Levin had abruptly departed, the princess was delighted, and said to her husband triumphantly: "You see I was right." When Vronsky appeared on the scene, she was still more delighted, confirmed in her opinion that Kitty was to make not simply a good, but a brilliant match.

In the mother's eyes there could be no comparison between Vronsky and Levin. She disliked in Levin his strange and uncompromising opinions and his shyness in society, founded, as she supposed, on his pride and his queer sort of life, as she considered it, absorbed in cattle and peasants. She did not very much like it that he, who was in love with her daughter, had kept coming to the house for six weeks, as though he were waiting for something, inspecting, as though he were afraid he might be doing them too great an honor by making an offer, and did not realize that a man, who continually visits at a house where there is a young unmarried girl, is bound to make his intentions clear. And suddenly, without doing so, he disappeared. "It's as well he's not attractive enough for Kitty to have fallen in love with him," thought the mother.

Vronsky satisfied all the mother's desires. Very wealthy, clever, of aristocratic family, on the highroad to a brilliant career in the army and at court, and a fascinating man. Nothing better could be wished for.

Vronsky openly flirted with Kitty at balls, danced with her, and came continually to the house, consequently there could be no doubt of the seriousness of his intentions. But, in spite of that, the mother had spent the whole of that winter in a state of terrible anxiety and agitation.

Princess Shtcherbatskaya had herself been married thirty years ago, her aunt arranging the match. Her husband, about whom everything was well known before hand, had come, looked at his future bride, and been looked at. The match-making aunt had ascertained and communicated their mutual impression. That impression had been favorable. Afterwards, on a day fixed beforehand, the expected offer was made to her parents, and accepted. All had passed very simply and easily. So it seemed, at least, to the princess. But over her own daughters she had felt how far from simple and easy is the business, apparently so commonplace, of marrying off one's daughters. The panics that had been lived through, the thoughts that had been brooded over, the money that had been wasted, and the disputes with her husband over marrying the two elder girls, Darya and Natalia! Now, since the youngest had come out, she was going through the same terrors, the same doubts, and still more violent quarrels with her husband than she had over the elder girls. The old prince, like all fathers indeed, was exceedingly punctilious on the score of the honor and reputation of his daughters. He was irrationally jealous over his daughters, especially over Kitty, who was his favorite. At every turn he had scenes with the princess for compromising her daughter. The princess had grown accustomed to this already with her other daughters, but now she felt that there was more ground for the prince's touchiness. She saw that of late years much was changed in the manners of society, that a mother's duties had become still more difficult. She saw that girls of Kitty's age formed some sort of clubs, went to some sort of lectures, mixed freely in men's society; drove about the streets alone, many of them did not curtsey, and, what was the most important thing, all the girls were firmly convinced that to choose their husbands was their own affair, and not their parents'. "Marriages aren't made nowadays as they used to be," was thought and said by all these young girls, and even by their elders. But how marriages were made now, the princess could not learn from any one. The French fashion—of the parents arranging their children's future—was not accepted; it was condemned. The English fashion of the complete independence of girls was also not accepted, and not possible in Russian society. The Russian fashion of match-making by the offices of intermediate persons was for some reason considered unseemly; it was ridiculed by every one, and by the princess herself. But how girls were to be married, and how parents were to marry them, no one knew. Everyone with whom the princess had chanced to discuss the matter said the same thing: "Mercy on us, it's high time in our day to cast off all that old-fashioned business. It's the young people have to marry; and not their parents; and so we ought to leave the young people to arrange it as they choose." It was very easy for anyone to say that who had no daughters, but the princess realized that in the process of getting to know each other, her daughter might fall in love, and fall in love with someone who did not care to marry her or who was quite unfit to be her husband. And, however much it was instilled into the princess that in our times young people ought to arrange their lives for themselves, she was unable to believe it, just as she would have been unable to believe that, at any time whatever, the most suitable playthings for children five years old ought to be loaded pistols. And so the princess was more uneasy over Kitty than she had been over her elder sisters.

Now she was afraid that Vronsky might confine himself to simply flirting with her daughter. She saw that her daughter was in love with him, but tried to comfort herself with the thought that he was an honorable man, and would not do this. But at the same time she knew how easy it is, with the freedom of manners of today, to turn a girl's head, and how lightly men generally regard such a crime. The week before, Kitty had told her mother of a conversation she had with Vronsky during a mazurka. This conversation had partly reassured the princess; but perfectly at ease she could not be. Vronsky had told Kitty that both he and his brother were so used to obeying their mother that they never made up their minds to any important undertaking without consulting her. "And just now, I am impatiently awaiting my mother's arrival from Petersburg, as peculiarly fortunate," he told her.

Kitty had repeated this without attaching any significance to the words. But her mother saw them in a different light. She knew that the old lady was expected from day to day, that she would be pleased at her son's choice, and she felt it strange that he should not make his offer through fear of vexing his mother. However, she was so anxious for the marriage itself, and still more for relief from her fears, that she believed it was so. Bitter as it was for the princess to see the unhappiness of her eldest daughter, Dolly, on the point of leaving her husband, her anxiety over the decision of her youngest daughter's fate engrossed all her feelings. Today, with Levin's reappearance, a fresh source of anxiety arose. She was afraid that her daughter, who had at one time, as she fancied, a feeling for Levin, might, from extreme sense of honor, refuse Vronsky, and that Levin's arrival might generally complicate and delay the affair so near being concluded.

"Why, has he been here long?" the princess asked about Levin, as they returned home.

"He came today, mamma."

"There's one thing I want to say..." began the princess, and from her serious and alert face, Kitty guessed what it would be.

"Mamma," she said, flushing hotly and turning quickly to her, "please, please don't say anything about that. I know, I know all about it."

She wished for what her mother wished for, but the motives of her mother's wishes wounded her.

"I only want to say that to raise hopes..."

"Mamma, darling, for goodness' sake, don't talk about it. It's so horrible to talk about it."

"I won't," said her mother, seeing the tears in her daughter's eyes; "but one thing, my love; you promised me you would have no secrets from me. You won't?"

"Never, mamma, none," answered Kitty, flushing a little, and looking her mother straight in the face, "but there's no use in my telling you anything, and I...I...if I wanted to, I don't know what to say or how...I don't know..."

"No, she could not tell an untruth with those eyes," thought the mother, smiling at her agitation and happiness. The princess smiled that what was taking place just now in her soul seemed to the poor child so immense and so important.

16. What is one difference between Levin and Count Vronsky?
    a. Levin is shy and Count Vronsky has uncompromising opinions.
    b. Levin is focused on life in the countryside while Count Vronsky has an aristocratic background.
    c. Levin has uncompromising opinions while Count Vronsky is absorbed by cattle and peasants.
    d. Levin is wealthy while Count Vronsky comes from an aristocratic family.

17. Read the following dictionary entry.
    Fancy v. 1. To be interested in 2. To imagine something 3. To believe something that may or may not be true 4. To interpret something
Which definition best matches the way the word *fancied* is used in paragraph 8?
    a. Definition 1
    b. Definition 2
    c. Definition 3
    d. Definition 4

18. This story is set in Russia. Why is the location important to the story?
    a. Princess Kitty is only interested in marrying a Russian
    b. Princess Kitty will be matched according to the Russian style of using a matchmaker
    c. The characters are, in part, shaped by their national heritage
    d. Princess Kitty ultimately rebels against Russian society by choosing a husband using the English method

19. What is the likely importance of Vronsky's mother's arrival?
    a. Vronsky is going to introduce his mother to Princess Kitty.
    b. Vronsky is going to take his mother to a Moscow ball.
    c. Vronsky is going to ask his mother if he should marry Kitty.
    d. Vronsky is going to show his mother around Moscow.

20. In paragraph 6, the word *punctilious* most likely means:
    a. careful
    b. punctual
    c. on time
    d. jealous

21. Which sentence or phrase best demonstrates that customs in Moscow have changed?
    a. The panics that had been lived through, the thoughts that had been brooded over, the money that had been wasted, and the disputes with her husband over marrying the two elder girls, Darya and Natalia!
    b. She saw that girls of Kitty's age formed some sort of clubs, went to some sort of lectures, mixed freely in men's society
    c. The French fashion—of the parents arranging their children's future—was not accepted
    d. And so the princess was more uneasy over Kitty than she had been over her elder sisters.

22. In paragraph 7, Kitty's mother is concerned that Kitty might marry someone who is *unfit to be her husband*. What characteristic is Kitty's mother mostly like to think makes a suitor unfit?
   a. Shyness
   b. A member of the aristocracy
   c. Cleverness
   d. Obedient

23. The author uses paragraph 1 to:
   a. introduce Princess Kitty's mother
   b. introduce the central conflict of the passage
   c. describe the Moscow balls
   d. describe Levin and Count Vronsky

Questions 24 – 30 pertain to the following passages:

Great Britain and Her Queen
By Anne E. Keeling

Chapter I
The Girl-Queen and Her Kingdom

Rather more than one mortal lifetime, as we average life in these later days, has elapsed since that June morning of 1837, when Victoria of England, then a fair young princess of eighteen, was roused from her tranquil sleep in the old palace at Kensington, and bidden to rise and meet the Primate, and his dignified associates the Lord Chamberlain and the royal physician, who "were come on business of state to the Queen"—words of startling import, for they meant that, while the royal maiden lay sleeping, the aged King, whose heiress she was, had passed into the deeper sleep of death. It is already an often-told story how promptly, on receiving that summons, the young Queen rose and came to meet her first homagers, standing before them in hastily assumed wrappings, her hair hanging loosely, her feet in slippers, but in all her hearing such royally firm composure as deeply impressed those heralds of her greatness, who noticed at the same moment that her eyes were full of tears. This little scene is not only charming and touching, it is very significant, suggesting a combination of such qualities as are not always found united: sovereign good sense and readiness, blending with quick, artless feeling that sought no disguise—such feeling as again betrayed itself when on her ensuing proclamation the new Sovereign had to meet her people face to face, and stood before them at her palace window, composed but sad, the tears running unchecked down her fair pale face.

That rare spectacle of simple human emotion, at a time when a selfish or thoughtless spirit would have leaped in exultation, touched the heart of England deeply, and was rightly held of happy omen. The nation's feeling is aptly expressed in the glowing verse of Mrs. Browning, praying Heaven's blessing on the "weeping Queen," and prophesying for her the love, happiness, and honour which have been hers in no stinted measure. "Thou shalt be well beloved," said the poetess; there are very few sovereigns of whom it could be so truly said that they *have* been well beloved, for not many have so well deserved it. The faith of the singer has been amply justified, as time has made manifest the rarer qualities joyfully divined in those early days in the royal child, the single darling hope of the nation.

Once before in the recent annals of our land had expectations and desires equally ardent centred themselves on one young head. Much of the loyal devotion which had been alienated from the immediate family of George III had transferred itself to his grandchild, the Princess Charlotte, sole offspring of the unhappy marriage between George, Prince of Wales, and Caroline of Brunswick. The people had watched with vivid interest the young romance of Princess Charlotte's happy marriage, and had bitterly lamented her too early death—an event which had overshadowed all English hearts with forebodings of disaster. Since that dark day a little of the old attachment of England to its sovereigns had revived for the frank-mannered sailor and "patriot king," William IV; but the hopes crushed by the death of the much-regretted Charlotte had renewed themselves with even better warrant for Victoria. She was the child of no ill-omened, miserable marriage, but of a fitting union; her parents had been sundered only by death, not by wretched domestic dissensions. People heard that the mortal malady which deprived her of a father had been brought about by the Duke of Kent's simple delight in his baby princess, which kept him playing with the child when he should have been changing his wet outdoor garb; and they found something touching and tender in the tragic little circumstance. And everything that could be noticed of the manner in which the bereaved duchess was training up her precious charge spoke well for the mother's wisdom and affection, and for the future of the daughter.

It was indeed a happy day for England when Edward, Duke of Kent, the fourth son of George III, was wedded to Victoria of Saxe-Coburg, the widowed Princess of Leiningen—happy, not only because of the admirable skill with which that lady conducted her illustrious child's education, and because of the pure, upright principles, the frank, noble character, which she transmitted to that child, but because the family connection established through that marriage was to be yet further serviceable to the interests of our realm. Prince Albert of Saxe-Coburg was second son of the Duchess of Kent's eldest brother, and thus first cousin of the Princess Victoria—"the Mayflower," as, in fond allusion to the month of her birth, her mother's kinsfolk loved to call her: and it has been made plain that dreams of a possible union between the two young cousins, very nearly of an age, were early cherished by the elders who loved and admired both.

The Princess's life, however, was sedulously guarded from all disturbing influences. She grew up in healthy simplicity and seclusion; she was not apprised of her nearness to the throne till she was twelve years old; she had been little at Court, little in sight, but had been made familiar with her own land and its history, having received the higher education so essential to her great position; while simple truth and rigid honesty were the very atmosphere of her existence. From such a training much might be hoped; but even those who knew most and hoped most were not quite prepared for the strong individual character and power of self-determination that revealed themselves in the girlish being so suddenly transferred "from the nursery to the throne." It was quickly noticed that the part of Queen and mistress seemed native to her, and that she filled it with not more grace than propriety. "She always strikes me as possessed of singular penetration, firmness, and independence," wrote Dr. Norman Macleod in 1860; acute observers in 1837 took note of the same traits, rarer far in youth than in full maturity, and closely connected with the "reasoning, searching" quality of her mind, "anxious to get at the root and reality of things, and abhorring all shams, whether in word or deed."

It was well for England that its young Sovereign could exemplify virile strength as well as womanly sweetness; for it was indeed a cloudy and dark day when she was called to her post of lonely grandeur and hard responsibility; and to fill that post rightly would have overtasked and overwhelmed a feebler nature. It is true that the peace of Europe, won at Waterloo, was still unbroken. But already, within our borders and without them, there were the signs of coming storm. The condition of Ireland was chronically bad; the condition of England was full of danger; on the Continent a new period of earth-shaking revolution announced itself not doubtfully.

It would be hardly possible to exaggerate the wretched state of the sister isle, where fires of recent hate were still smouldering, and where the poor inhabitants, guilty and guiltless, were daily living on the verge of famine, over which they were soon to be driven. Their ill condition much aggravated by the intemperate habits to which despairing men so easily fall a prey. The expenditure of Ireland on proof spirits alone had in the year 1829 attained the sum of £6,000,000.

In England many agricultural labourers were earning starvation wages, were living on bad and scanty food, and were housed so wretchedly that they might envy the hounds their dry and clean kennels. A dark symptom of their hungry discontent had shown itself in the strange crime of rick-burning, which went on under cloud of night season after season, despite the utmost precautions which the luckless farmers could adopt. The perpetrators were not dimly guessed to be half-famished creatures, taking a mad revenge for their wretchedness by destroying the tantalising stores of grain, too costly for their consumption; the price of wheat in the early years of Her Majesty's reign and for some time previously being very high, and reaching at one moment (1847) the extraordinary figure of a hundred and two shillings per quarter.

There was threatening distress, too, in some parts of the manufacturing districts; in others a tolerably high level of wages indicated prosperity. But even in the more favoured districts there was needless suffering. The hours of work, unrestricted by law, were cruelly long; nor did there exist any restriction as to the employment of operatives of very tender years. "The cry of the children" was rising up to heaven, not from the factory only, but from the underground darkness of the mine, where a system of pitiless infant slavery prevailed, side by side with the employment of women as beasts of burden, "in an atmosphere of filth and profligacy." The condition of too many toilers was rendered more hopeless by the thriftless follies born of ignorance. The educational provision made by the piety of former ages was no longer adequate to the needs of the ever-growing nation; and all the voluntary efforts made by clergy and laity, by Churchmen and Dissenters, did not fill up the deficiency—a fact which had only just begun to meet with State recognition. It was in 1834 that Government first obtained from Parliament the grant of a small sum in aid of education. Under a defective system of poor-relief, recently reformed, an immense mass of idle pauperism had come into being; it still remained to be seen if a new Poor Law could do away with the mischief created by the old one.

Looking at the earliest years of Her Majesty's rule, the first impulse is to exclaim: "And all this trouble did not pass, but grew."

24. Which of these is not one of the immediate problems that faced the nation at the time that Victoria was crowned?
    a. Europe was not at war.
    b. The people in Ireland were suffering.
    c. Agricultural laborers were not earning enough money.
    d. There wasn't enough money for education.

25. What is Paragraph 3 mainly about?
    a. Victoria's childhood
    b. The royal family
    c. Victoria's cousin
    d. Victoria's father, the Duke of Kent

26. In paragraph 2, the author uses a quote from Mrs. Browning to show which of the below?
    a. Queen Victoria was not beloved
    b. Queen Victoria had a lot of happiness in her life
    c. Mrs. Browning accurately predicted the people's opinion about Queen Victoria
    d. Queen Victoria had a selfish and thoughtless spirit

27. The primary purpose of paragraphs 7-9 is to:
    a. illustrate Queen Victoria's first acts as queen
    b. show the poor conditions for workers in manufacturing districts
    c. show the problems faced by the people of Ireland
    d. describe the challenges faced by Victoria when she became queen

28. According to the author, what was one specific problem that resulted from the government's efforts to aid the poor?
    a. Poverty increased
    b. There wasn't enough money for education
    c. The trouble grew
    d. The system was reformed

29. What is one reason why Victoria's childhood was relatively simple?
    a. She spent much of her childhood with her cousin
    b. She didn't know she had a possibility of being queen until she was twelve
    c. She was very independent
    d. She received a lot of education

30. Which word or phrase from paragraph 9 best helps the reader understand the meaning of *tender years* in paragraph 9?
    a. Needless suffering
    b. Cruelly long
    c. Pitiless infant slavery
    d. Beasts of burden

Writing

Read the selection and answer the questions 1-5.

(1) In the early 1760s, Paul Revere, ran a busy metalworking shop. (2) People from all over Boston came to buy the silver and gold cups, medals, and cutlery he made. (3) Everything changed in 1765. (4) Many colonists ran low on money and stopped shopping at Paul's shop.

(5) Things got worse when the british passed the Stamp Act. (6) The Stamp Act created a tax to help the British earn money. (7) Colonists like Paul Revere hated the Stamp Act because it would make things more expensive.

(8) Under the Stamp Act, colonists needed to pay for everything that was printed, such as newspapers, magazines, and business contracts. (9) After a colonist paid the tax, the tax collector put a stamp on the paper to show that the tax had been paid.

(10) The Stamp Act made it very expensive for Paul to run his business. (11) For example, if he wanted a new apprentice for his silver shop, he needed to buy a Stamp for the signed contract.

(12) Paul wasn't just angry about buying stamps. (13) He also felt that the British shouldn't be allowed to tax the colonies. (14) There was no American colonists in the British parliament, which passed the tax. (15) Paul and the other colonists didn't want taxation without representation. (16) They wanted to be able to choose their own taxes.

(17) The colonists refused to buy stamps. (18) They were determined to get the Stamp Act repealed.

(19) Paul joined a group called the Sons of Liberty. (20) They wore silver medals on their coats that said "Sons of Liberty." (21) Paul may have helped make the medals in his silver shop.

(22) The Sons of Liberty staged demonstrations at the Liberty Tree, a huge elm tree, that stood in Boston. (23) Paul drew cartoons and wrote poems about liberty. (24) He published them in the local newspaper, *The Boston Gazette*.

(25) After a year of hard work fighting the Stamp Act Paul and the Sons of Liberty received the happy news. (26) The Stamp Act had been repealed!

(27) People celebrated all over Boston; they lit bonfires, set off fireworks, and decorated houses and ships with flags and streamers. (28) Paul attended the biggest celebration, which took place at the Liberty Tree. (29) The people hung 280 lanterns on the tree's branches lighting up the night sky.

(30) Some members of the Sons of Liberty constructed a paper obelisk. (31) An obelisk is the same shape as the Washington Monument. (32) They decorated the obelisk with pictures and verses about the struggle to repeal the Stamp Act and hung it from the Liberty Tree.

(33) Paul may have helped construct the obelisk, even if he wasn't involved in the direct construction, he probably knew about and supported it. (34) After the celebration, he made a copper engraving showing the pictures and verses on the obelisk's four sides. (35) His engraving records the celebration under the Liberty Tree. (36) Even though Paul Revere may be better known for his silver work and famous ride, his engravings, like the engraving of the obelisk, help us see the American Revolution through his eyes.

1. What change should be made to sentence 1?
    a. Change *1760s* to *1760's*
    b. Delete the comma after *1760s*
    c. Delete the comma after *Revere*
    d. Add a comma after *busy*

2. What change should be made to sentence 5?
    a. Change *got* to *get*
    b. Change *worse* to *worst*
    c. Change *british* to *British*
    d. Change *Stamp Act* to *stamp act*

3. What is the most effective way to combine sentences 30 and 31?
    a. Some members of the Sons of Liberty constructed a paper obelisk, which is the same shape as the Washington Monument.
    b. Some members of the Sons of Liberty constructed a paper obelisk which is the same shape as the Washington Monument.
    c. Some members of the Sons of Liberty constructed a paper obelisk, that is the same shape as the Washington Monument.
    d. Some members of the Sons of Liberty constructed a paper obelisk; which is the same shape as the Washington Monument.

4. What change should be made to sentence 14?
    a. Change *was* to *were*
    b. Change *parliament* to *parlaiment*
    c. Delete the comma after *parliament*
    d. Change *which* to *that*

5. What is the most effective way to combine sentences 17 and 18?
    a. The colonists refused to buy stamps and they were determined to get the Stamp Act repealed.
    b. The colonists refused to buy stamps, and they were determined to get the Stamp Act repealed.
    c. The colonists refused to buy stamps, and were determined to get the Stamp Act repealed.
    d. The colonists refused to buy stamps, were determined to get the Stamp Act repealed.

6. Which of the following sentences is correct?
    a. Sonja works very hard, she is tired all the time.
    b. Sonja works very hard she is tired all the time.
    c. Sonja works very hard, however, she is tired all the time.
    d. Sonja works very hard; she is tired all the time.

7. Choose the word that correctly fills the blank the following sentence:
Mrs. Simmons asked her students to get their books, read the first chapter, and _____ the questions at the end.
    a. answer
    b. to answer
    c. answering
    d. will answer

8. Choose the correct spelling of the word that fills the blank in the following sentence:
Plastic trash that ends up in the ocean can have a _____, or harmful, effect on marine life.
    a. diliterious
    b. deleterious
    c. delaterious
    d. dilaterious

9. Which of the following choices best defines the underlined word?
The impoverished shepherds stumbled upon the <u>stele</u> while desperately searching for some lost sheep; they were surprised and puzzled by the bizarre lines and squiggles that covered its face.
    a. an item that has been looted from a tomb
    b. a sign that indicates direction
    c. the side of cliff
    d. a large, inscribed stone

10. Which of the following words is NOT spelled correctly?
    a. aggregate
    b. mischiefs
    c. subservient
    d. ought

11. Which of the following choices best completes the selection below?
The letter _____ explained all his hopes and dreams for my success; _____ outpouring of his love for me.
    a. my grandfather, it contained an
    b. from my grandfather, which containing
    c. grandfather, since it contained
    d. from my grandfather, it contained an

12. Which of the following choices is correct?
    a. Whether the unexamined life is worth living or not; there is little doubt that people who do not carefully consider their actions often fall into difficulties.
    b. There are basically two ways to live: with your conscience or moral code, which can be a difficult and painful road; or against your conscience, which may seem easy and attractive until you discover how much pain and suffering you've caused others.
    c. Folding the paper over carefully so the contents were in full view; Caroline, fearful of what was coming next in the article, leaned closer to the printed page in order to more fully absorb the awful truths contained there.
    d. It is unnecessary to become a philosopher to take a careful look at your existence to understand the nature of it; its application; its fundamental principles, and its future.

13. Which of the following words is NOT spelled correctly?
    a. onomatopoeia
    b. fastidious
    c. meticulus
    d. minutiae

14. What is the meaning of the underlined word?
> *The girls sat at the table, comforting each other and sobbing through* <u>lachrymose</u> *stories about their own struggles with bad haircuts.*
   a. consolatory
   b. blithe
   c. mournful
   d. lethargic

15. Which of the following choices best completes the sentence?
_____, there's no way you will be able to be a part of the swimming relay competition.
   a. Unless you find a new partner
   b. You have a new partner
   c. When it is time
   d. As you can find a partner

16. Which of the following choices shows the best way to punctuate the sentence?
   a. I packed a picnic to take to the park with my friends; I made sure that I brought all of the plates and cups, too.
   b. I packed a picnic to take to the park with my friends, I made sure that I brought all of the plates and cups, too.
   c. I packed a picnic to take to the park with my friends I made sure that I brought all of the plates and cups, too.
   d. I packed a picnic to take to the park with my friends: I made sure that I brought all of the plates and cups, too.

17. Which of the following words is spelled incorrectly?
   a. salubrious
   b. surreptitious
   c. artifice
   d. requisition

18. Using the context of the selection below, what is the meaning of the underlined word?
The discussion over the new park had begun well, but it soon descended into an <u>acrimonious</u> debate over misuse of tax revenues.
   a. shocking
   b. childish
   c. rancorous
   d. revealing

19. To temporarily postpone repayment of a loan is to
   a. decry
   b. defer
   c. differ
   d. debtor

20. Which of the following choices best completes the sentence?

Natalie reviewed the notes carefully, with one eye on the judge's _____ and another eye on the _____ of the decision. There was certainly more than one way to _____ the case.

    a. interpretation, evolve, interpret
    b. interpretation, evolution, interpret
    c. interpret, evolution, interpretation
    d. interpretation, evolution, interpretation

21. The melody in that pop song is reminiscent of the one Beethoven used in the first movement of his ninth symphony?

Based on how it is used in the sentence, the word <u>reminiscent</u> means

    a. superior
    b. suggestive
    c. situated
    d. synonymous

22. Read the following introduction from an essay about Mary Shelley.

Mary Shelley conceived of Dr. Frankenstein and the hideous monster he created, which helped the English novelist to make an immeasurable impact on literature and popular culture.

Which of the following statements most effectively revises this introduction?

    a. English novelist Mary Shelley had an immeasurable impact on literature and popular culture when she conceived of Dr. Frankenstein and the hideous monster he created.
    b. Dr. Frankenstein created a hideous monster, and they were conceived by English novelist Mary Shelley, who had an immeasurable impact on literature and popular culture.
    c. English novelist Mary Shelley conceived of Dr. Frankenstein and the hideous monster he created and had an immeasurable impact on literature and popular culture.
    d. Novelist Mary Shelley from England had an immeasurable impact on literature and popular culture when she conceived of Dr. Frankenstein and the hideous monster he created.

23. According to Merriam-Webster's Dictionary, what is the correct pronunciation of the word "impromptu?"

    a. \im-promp-too
    b. \imp-römp-tu
    c. \im-'präm(p)-(,)tü
    d. \im-prömpt-ü

24. Read the following introduction from an essay about automobiles.

A valuable tool for crossing long distances the automobile is a friend, and perpetrator of toxic pollution, the automobile is a foe.

What is the MOST effective revision of this introduction?

    a. The automobile crosses long distances, which is a good thing, but it is also a perpetrator of toxic pollution, which is bad.
    b. Both a valuable tool for crossing long distances and a perpetrator of toxic pollution, the automobile is both friend and foe.
    c. Automobiles are good because they help us cross long distances, but they are bad because they create a lot of pollution.
    d. Both a valuable tool for crossing long distances— the automobile is both friend and foe— and perpetrator of toxic pollution.

25. Read the following line from a speech arguing in favor of a road repair.
Repairing route 211 will save members of this community a lot of money.
Which of the following is the BEST follow-up statement?
    a. Also the potholes that run the entire length of route 211 are unpleasant to look at.
    b. Another road that requires a great deal of attention in this community is Central Highway.
    c. Last year, local drivers spent over $16,000 to repair damages caused by potholes in the road.
    d. During economically uncertain times, financial matters are at the forefront of all Americans' concerns.

26. According to Merriam-Webster's Dictionary, which word derives from the English word fawney, which was a gilded brass ring?
    a. fawning
    b. phone
    c. phony
    d. fallen

27. Mara enjoyed great felicity when her missing dog found his way home.
What does the word "felicity" mean in this sentence?
    a. Discomfort
    b. Anxiety
    c. Disbelief
    d. Happiness

28. Choose the word that best fills the blank in the following sentence:
Stanley had never liked Nathan, but he grudgingly _____ Nathan for his idea of holding a car wash for the school fundraiser.
    a. exalted
    b. praised
    c. honored
    d. commended

29. The detective dedicated his life to hunting down the truth.
What does "hunting down the truth" mean in this sentence?
    a. The detective preferred to work with a gun.
    b. The detective was determined to tell the truth.
    c. The detective wanted to eradicate the truth.
    d. The detective was determined to learn the truth.

30. Choose the sentence that most effectively follows the conventions of Standard Written English:
    a. Betty MacDonald became famous for her first novel, *The Egg and I*, which chronicles her adventures in chicken farming.
    b. *The Egg and I*, a book written by Betty MacDonald, made the author famous and chronicled her adventures in chicken farming.
    c. Betty MacDonald wrote *The Egg and I*, and became famous chronicling her adventures in chicken farming.
    d. *The Egg and I* chronicles the author's adventures in chicken farming, and made Betty MacDonald famous.

Answers and Explanations

Mathematics

1. A: The expression may be factored as $(x - 8)(x + 5)$. The factorization may be checked by distributing each term in the first factor over each term in the second factor. Doing so gives $x^2 + 5x - 8x - 40$, which can be rewritten as $x^2 - 3x - 40$.

2. C: The denominator may be factored as $(x + 8)(x - 4)$. Therefore, the expression can be rewritten as $\frac{x-4}{(x+8)(x-4)}$, which reduces to $\frac{1}{x+8}$.

3. B: The denominator may be factored as $(x^2 - 9)(x - 6)$. The first binomial may be factored as $(x - 3)(x + 3)$. Thus, the given expression may be rewritten as $\frac{x-3}{(x-3)(x+3)(x-6)}$, which simplifies to $\frac{1}{(x+3)(x-6)}$.

4. C: The power to which 2 is raised to give 64 is 6; $2^6 = 64$. Thus, $x = 6$.

5. C: The least common denominator of $x(x + 4)$ may be multiplied by both rational expressions. Doing so gives $2x = 3(x + 4)$ or $2x = 3x + 12$. Solving for x gives $x = -12$.

6. B: To factor the polynomial, find factors of the first and third term whose product can be added to get the middle term. The fastest way to find the correct answer is to multiply the answer choices and select the choice that yields the original equation. In this case,

$$(x + 5)(2x - 3) = (x)(2x) + (x)(-3) + (5)(2x) + (5)(-3)$$
$$= 2x^2 - 3x + 10x - 15$$
$$= 2x^2 + 7x - 15$$

7. C: The solution to the equation follows:

$$x^2 - 9 = 0$$
$$x^2 = 9$$
$$x = \sqrt{9}$$
$$x = +3 \text{ and } x = -3$$

8. D: Write the equation in slope-intercept form: $y = mx + b$ where m is the slope of the line and b is the y-intercept. In this case, the slope m = 10 and the y-intercept b = -15. Hence $y = 10x - 15$.

9. C: At the intersection point of line 1 and line 2, $y_1 = y_2 = y$ and $x_1 = x_2 = x$. To find the x coordinate, let $y_1 = y_2$.

$$2x + 6 = -x - 3$$
$$2x + x = -6 - 3$$
$$3x = -9$$
$$x = -3$$

10. C: The inequality that best represents the number of questions Joshua must answer correctly is $23 < x \leq 30$. Hence, the left endpoint of the graph is 23, and the right endpoint is 30. Because Joshua must answer more than 23 questions, the endpoint at 23 is not included in the data set and is represented by an open circle.

11. C: To simplify the expression, first simplify the expression with parentheses. To raise $2x$ to the third power, raise both 2 and x to the third power separately.
$$x^5 \cdot (2x)^3 = x^5 \cdot 2^3 \cdot x^3$$
$$= x^5 \cdot 8x^3$$
Next, multiply the terms. Since they have the same base and are being multiplied together, add the exponents to the like base.
$$x^5 \cdot 8x^3 = 8x^{5+3}$$
$$= 8x^8$$

12. A: You can solve the quadratic inequality using graphs, tables, or algebraic methods. For this explanation, we will approach the problem algebraically. To begin, rewrite the equation in form $ax^2 + bx + c = 0$ by subtracting 8 from both sides.
$$3x^2 + 4x = 8$$
$$3x^2 + 4x - 8 = 0$$
The left side cannot be factored, so we will have to use the quadratic formula to solve the equation. For the variables in the quadratic formula, use $a = 3$, $b = 4$, and $c = -8$.
$$x = \frac{-b \pm \sqrt{b^2 - 4ac}}{2a}$$
$$= \frac{-4 \pm \sqrt{16 - (-96)}}{6}$$
$$= \frac{-4 \pm \sqrt{112}}{6}$$
$$= \frac{-4 \pm 4\sqrt{7}}{6}$$
$$= -\frac{4}{6} \pm \frac{4\sqrt{7}}{6}$$
$$= -\frac{2}{3} \pm \frac{2}{3}\sqrt{7}$$

13. B: To simplify the expression, first factor the numerator and the denominator. To factor the numerator, use trial-and-error to find two numbers whose sum is 2 and whose product is -24, and then put those numbers into the form $(x + \_)(x + \_)$. For the denominator, factor out the common factor, which is 5.
$$\frac{x^2 + 2x - 24}{5x - 20} = \frac{(x+6)(x-4)}{5(x-4)}$$
Now there is a common factor, $(x - 4)$, in both the numerator and the denominator. Therefore, you can further simplify the expression by cancelling it out.
$$\frac{(x+6)(x-4)}{5(x-4)} = \frac{x+6}{5}$$

14. C: To simplify the expression, first simplify the expression with parentheses. To raise $3x$ to the third power, raise both 3 and x to the third power separately.
$$x^6 \cdot (3x)^2 = x^6 \cdot 3^2 \cdot x^2$$
$$= x^6 \cdot 9x^2$$
Next, multiply the two terms. Since they have the same base and are being multiplied together, add the exponents of the like base, x.
$$x^6 \cdot 9x^2 = 9x^{6+2}$$
$$= 9x^8$$

15. C: The left side of the equation cannot be factored, so use the quadratic equation. Remember that the square root of a negative number is an imaginary number.

$$x = \frac{-b \pm \sqrt{b^2 - 4ac}}{2a}$$
$$= \frac{-4 \pm \sqrt{16 - 32}}{2}$$
$$= \frac{-4 \pm \sqrt{-16}}{2}$$
$$= \frac{-4 \pm 4i}{2}$$
$$= -\frac{4}{2} \pm \frac{4i}{2}$$
$$= -2 \pm 2i$$

16. B: The left side of the equation cannot be factored, so use the quadratic equation. Remember that the square root of a negative number is an imaginary number.

$$x = \frac{-b \pm \sqrt{b^2 - 4ac}}{2a}$$
$$= \frac{3 \pm \sqrt{9 - 84}}{6}$$
$$= \frac{3 \pm \sqrt{-75}}{6}$$
$$= \frac{3 \pm 5i\sqrt{3}}{6}$$
$$= \left(\frac{3}{6}\right) \pm \left(\frac{5i\sqrt{3}}{6}\right)$$
$$= \frac{1}{2} \pm \frac{5i}{6}\sqrt{3}$$

17. D: You can solve the rational equation using graphs, tables, or algebraic methods. For this explanation, we will approach the problem algebraically. To begin, get rid of the denominators by multiplying both sides by $x(x + 2)$, and then simplify the result.

$$\frac{5}{x} - \frac{6}{x+2} = 1$$
$$x(x + 2) \cdot \left(\frac{5}{x} - \frac{6}{x+2}\right) = x(x + 2) \cdot 1$$
$$5(x + 2) - 6(x) = x(x + 2)$$
$$5x + 10 - 6x = x^2 + 2x$$
$$x^2 + 3x - 10 = 0$$

The result is a quadratic equation. Solve it by factoring the left side.

$$(x + 5)(x - 2) = 0$$
$$x = -5 \text{ and } x = 2$$

Therefore, the possible solutions are $x = -5$ and $x = 2$. Unfortunately, whenever you solve a rational equation in this manner, you run the risk of finding an incorrect solution. Consequently, we cannot automatically say that the solutions are $x = -5$ and $x = 2$. Check the solutions by, substituting them into the given equations and making sure that the result is a true statement.

$x = -5$:
$$\left(\frac{5}{-5}\right) - \left(\frac{6}{-5+2}\right) = 1$$
$$-\left(\frac{5}{5}\right) - \left(\frac{6}{-3}\right) = 1$$
$$-1 + 2 = 1 \text{ True}$$

$x = 2$:
$$\left(\frac{5}{2}\right) - \left(\frac{6}{2+2}\right) = 1$$
$$\left(\frac{5}{2}\right) - \left(\frac{6}{4}\right) = 1$$
$$\left(\frac{5}{2}\right) - \left(\frac{3}{2}\right) = 1$$
$$\left(\frac{2}{2}\right) = 1 \text{ True}$$

Therefore, the solutions are x=-5 and x=2.

18. B: You can solve the rational equation using graphs, tables, or algebraic methods. For this explanation, we will approach the problem algebraically. To begin, factor the polynomials in the numerator and denominator.

$$\frac{x^2+5x-6}{x^2-1} = 2$$

$$\frac{(x+6)(x-1)}{(x+1)(x-1)} = 2$$

Notice that the expression $x - 1$ appears in both the numerator and denominator. Therefore, you can cancel it from each as long as x is not 1. (That would make the denominator zero, which is undefined). After cancelling the common expression, multiply both sides by the new denominator $x + 1$ and solve

$$\frac{x+6}{x+1} = 2$$
$$x + 6 = 2(x + 1)$$
$$x + 6 = 2x + 2$$
$$x = 4$$

Thus, the solution is $x = 4$. Check this solution on your own by substituting it into the original equation and make sure that the result is a true statement.

19. C: The total number of small squares is 16, and 10 of them are shaded. To find a percentage divide 10 by 16: 10/16= .625, then multiply by 100 to make it a percent: 62.5%

20. B: "Percent" means "parts per 100". Setting the unknown number equal to x, this gives $\frac{30}{100}x = 18$. To solve this, isolate the variable by multiplying both sides of the equation by 100 and dividing both sides by 30, resulting in $x = (18)(\frac{100}{30}) = \frac{1800}{30} = 60$.

21. B: Substitute each of the given values for x and y into the equation. This yields $4^2 - (2 \times 3 - 3) = 16 - 3 = 13$.

22. C: The rules of exponents can be applied in order to rewrite the expression as: $-4q^3r^2s^{-1}$, which equals $\frac{-4q^3r^2}{s}$, or $-4\frac{q^3r^2}{s}$.

23. A: A line, given in the form, $y = mx + b$, has m as the slope and b as the y-intercept. In the linear equation, $y = 17x - 4$, 17 is the slope of the line.

24. B: The left side of the equation cannot be factored, so use the quadratic equation. Remember that the square root of a negative number is an imaginary number.

$$x = \frac{-b \pm \sqrt{b^2 - 4ac}}{2a}$$
$$= \frac{2 \pm \sqrt{4 - 112}}{4}$$
$$= \frac{2 \pm \sqrt{-108}}{4}$$
$$= \frac{2 \pm 6i\sqrt{3}}{4}$$
$$= \frac{2}{4} \pm \frac{6i\sqrt{3}}{4}$$
$$= \frac{1}{2} \pm \frac{3i}{2}\sqrt{3}$$

25. C: The linear equation can be rewritten as $y = -\frac{2}{3}x + \frac{7}{3}$. The slope-intercept form of an equation, or $y = mx + b$, includes m as the slope and b as the y-intercept. Therefore, the y-intercept of the equation is $\frac{7}{3}$.

26. B: To simplify the expression, first factor the numerator and the denominator. To factor the numerator, use trial-and-error to find two numbers whose sum is -3 and whose product is -18, and then put those numbers into the form $(x + \_)(x + \_)$. For the denominator, factor out the common factor, which is 5.

$$\frac{x^2 - 3x - 18}{5x - 30} = \frac{(x+3)(x-6)}{5(x-6)}$$

Now there is a common factor, $(x - 6)$, which is in both the numerator and the denominator. Therefore, you can further simplify the expression by cancelling it out.

$$\frac{(x+3)(x-6)}{5(x-6)} = \frac{x+3}{5}$$

27. C: To simplify the expression, first simplify the expression with parentheses. To raise $2x$ to the third power, raise both 2 and x to the third power separately.

$$x^5 \cdot (2x)^3 = x^5 \cdot 2^3 \cdot x^3$$
$$= x^5 \cdot 8x^3$$

Next, multiply the terms. Since they have the same base and are being multiplied together, add the exponents to the like base.

$$x^5 \cdot 8x^3 = 8x^{5+3}$$
$$= 8x^8$$

28. C: The left side of the equation cannot be factored, so use the quadratic equation. Remember that the square root of a negative number is an imaginary number.

$$x = \frac{-b \pm \sqrt{b^2 - 4ac}}{2a}$$
$$= \frac{-2 \pm \sqrt{4 - 40}}{2}$$
$$= \frac{-2 \pm \sqrt{-36}}{2}$$
$$= \frac{-2 \pm 6i}{2}$$
$$= -\frac{2}{2} \pm \frac{6i}{2}$$
$$= -1 \pm 3i$$

29. B: To factor the polynomial, find factors of the first and third term whose product can be added to get the middle term. Here, the factors 7 and -8 have a product of -56, and when added together yield -1. Another way to find the correct answer is to multiply the answer choices and select the choice that yields the original equation. In this case:

$$(x + 7)(x - 8) = (x)(x) + (x)(-8) + (7)(x) + (7)(-8)$$
$$= x^2 - 8x + 7x - 56$$
$$= x^2 - x - 56$$

30. C: To simplify the polynomial, group and combine all terms of the same order.

$$4x^3 + 5x - x^3 + 2x^2 + 17 - 3x^3 + 5x - 2x^2 + 3$$
$$(4x^3 - x^3 - 3x^3) + (2x^2 - 2x^2) + (5x + 5x) + (17 + 3)$$
$$0 + 0 + 10x + 20$$
$$10(x + 2)$$

Reading

1. B: The passage was written to analyze the works by Chang-Rae Lee and the themes presented in his most famous novels.

2. A: The author of this passage uses the first line of the novel to provide an example of one of the themes of the novel.

3. D: Espionage is part of the plot of the novel <u>Native Speaker</u>, but it is not a theme that recurs in Lee's works.

4. C: The passage states that Lee's interests in cultural identity and race emerge from his own experiences with these issues as a young immigrant to America.

5. A: The tone of the last paragraph suggests concern over the preservation of cultural identities in an increasingly mixed and expanding world.

6. A: Emma's life had been marked by the comfort of consistency, a close relationship with Miss Taylor, and the knowledge she tended to get her own way. Miss Taylor's marriage upset that comfort and consistency because a major aspect of Emma's life will change. Emma was afraid her intellect would be stifled without Miss Taylor, so she did not approach the change as an opportunity for possible intellectual growth.

7. D: The author uses words such as comfortable and happy to describe Emma's first twenty-one years. During this time, little vexed her. Based on this context, you can conclude that vex has the opposite meaning of words such as comfortable and happy. The answer choice most different from these positive words is displease.

8. C: The author states that Emma possessed the "power of having rather too much her own way," and instead of feeling happy for her recently married friend, she felt sorry for herself. These descriptions characterize Emma as selfish. Emma may consider herself unfortunate following Miss Taylor's marriage, but a lifetime of privilege and having her own way hardly makes her an unfortunate character. While Emma may indeed prove to be devious, this excerpt offers no evidence of deviousness. Although Emma seems to value intellectual interaction, nothing in the excerpt implies that she is particularly studious.

9. B: A product of upper-class privilege, Emma has grown accustomed always to getting her way. When Miss Taylor's marriage disrupts this aspect of her life, Emma cannot deal with the situation in a mature fashion and instead sinks into self-pity and sorrow. Although Emma cannot enjoy Miss Taylor's happiness upon her wedding because Emma is so wrapped up in her own feelings, this does not mean she feels neither kindness nor love for her friend.

10. B: The color black is often used figuratively to suggest badness. Emma is sad about Miss Taylor's wedding, and enduring the event has become nothing more than "black work" to her. Perhaps she pretends she is happy about the wedding, but no evidence in this excerpt suggests this conclusion. In addition, no evidence in the excerpt suggests that Emma organized the wedding. The author does not use "black" as a literal color in this excerpt, and no evidence in the excerpt suggests the wedding party wears black clothing.

11. D: By beginning his argument with an immediate criticism of the existing federal government, he immediately portrays it as a system in need of improvement. By presenting the government's inefficacy in no uncertain terms, Hamilton assumes the reader will take his claim at face value and be convinced of his subsequent argument for improvements. Hamilton only criticizes the federal government explicitly; he does not criticize the Constitution.

12. A: By addressing the reader directly and uniting himself with the reader by using words such as "we," Hamilton is establishing a sense of agreement between himself and the reader. By doing so he wants the reader to believe he and the reader share the same desires for and concerns about America. The first-person point of view does not necessarily establish a friendly or informal tone.

13. C: Alexander Hamilton describes his opponents as loud and bitter in this sentence. Such words suggest a lack of rationality, self-control, and kindness. This word usage almost represents an attempt to portray his political opponents as less than human. As a result, Hamilton is seeking to strengthen his argument by suggesting those oppose his argument are angry and irrational.

14. B: In paragraph 3, Alexander Hamilton attacks politicians who fear any change to the Constitution that might diminish their power. Although this attack may be central to his argument, Hamilton does not want to leave the reader with a bitter taste that Hamilton's sole reason for writing is to attack his opponents. Ironically, he then continues his attacks for the remainder of the excerpt.

15. A: According to the writer, a tyrant would pay his or her court to go along with everything he demands. The court then would be in a submissive position to the tyrant, an all-powerful ruler. Based on this context, you can conclude that "obsequious" and "submissive" share the same meaning.

16. B: because the passage says in paragraph 3 that Levin is absorbed in cattle and peasants, which can be found in the countryside. Paragraph 4 states that Vronsky comes from an aristocratic background, or family. While it's true that Levin is shy, choice A is incorrect because Levin is the character who has uncompromising opinions, not Vronsky. Choice C is incorrect because it is Levin who is absorbed by cattle and peasants, not Vronsky. Choice D is incorrect because paragraph 4 states that Vronsky is wealthy, not Levin.

17. C: because the context of the sentence shows that Kitty's mother believed, or fancied, that Kitty had feelings for Levin. While it might also be true that Kitty fancies (or is interested in Levin), choice A is incorrect because the structure of the sentence shows that *fancied* is used to show the mother's opinion. Choice C is incorrect because Kitty's mother is not imagining Kitty's feelings; based on Kitty's behavior earlier, she believes that Kitty was in love with Levin. Choice D is incorrect because Kitty's mother is not interpreting current events; instead, she fancies that Kitty had feelings for Levin based on her observations of Kitty's past behavior.

18. C: is the correct answer because Kitty's mother is torn by the changes that are reshaping her society. The reader can best understand the impact of these changes by understanding original Russian society, which is partly explained in paragraphs 1 and 6. Choice A is incorrect because the passage does not present evidence that Kitty is only interested in marrying a Russian; while this may be true, the passage does not indicate Kitty's feelings. Choice B is incorrect because paragraph 6 states that the Russian style of matchmaking was unseemly and no longer used. Choice D is

incorrect because the reader does not yet know whom Kitty marries and whether Kitty used the English method by choosing her husband herself.

19. C: that Vronsky is going to ask his mother if he should marry Kitty. Paragraph 7 says that Vronsky never makes important decisions without consulting her, and her visit will be an opportunity for him to ask her important questions. Choice A is incorrect because the passage doesn't indicate that Kitty might meet Vronsky's mother. Choice B is incorrect because Vronsky attends balls to dance with Kitty, not his mother. While Vronsky might show his mother around Moscow, choice D is incorrect because the passage does not imply that this will happen.

20. A: because the rest of the sentence explains that Kitty's father is punctilious about his daughters' honor and reputation, which means that he's careful to guard them. Choice B is incorrect because *punctual* means to be on time, and the passage doesn't show Kitty's father attempting to arrive anywhere promptly. Choice C is incorrect because it has the same meaning as punctual. Choice D is incorrect because *jealous* is used in the following sentence and is used to show that he guards his daughters carefully.

21. B: because it gives specific details about new behaviors, such as forming clubs and going to lectures. Choice A is incorrect because it focuses on the stress Kitty's mother felt as her older daughters got married. Choice C is incorrect because it shows that the French fashion was not accepted; this means that Russian society has not changed to embrace the French fashion. Choice D is incorrect because it shows Kitty's mother increased unease but does not show why.

22. A: because paragraph 3 says that Kitty's mother dislikes Levin's shyness. Choices B and C are incorrect because these are the characteristics mentioned as positive traits that Vronsky has in paragraph 4. Even though Vronsky, the mother's favorite, is very obedient to his mother, Kitty's mother does say that this trait makes him unsuitable for Kitty. She is a little uneasy about this trait, but does not rule Vronsky out as an acceptable husband. Therefore, choice D is incorrect.

23. B: because the paragraph shows that the central conflict is Kitty's feelings about Levin and Vronsky. Choice A is incorrect because Kitty's mother is not mentioned in paragraph 1. Choice C is incorrect because the paragraph only mentions the balls but does not give any details. Choice D is incorrect because the reader only learns details about Levin and Vronsky in the following paragraphs, not in paragraph 1.

24. A: because paragraph 6 explains that the peace that came upon Europe after the battle of Waterloo was still unbroken; the continent was not at war. Choices B, C, and D are incorrect because paragraphs 7-9 explain that these choices were problems. Paragraph 7 talks about the problems in Ireland, paragraph 8 talks about the low, or starvation, wages earned by many agricultural workers, and paragraph 9 mentions the problems with the education system.

25. B: because the paragraph talks primarily about the royal family, such as George III and Princess Charlotte. This paragraph serves to partially explain how Victoria came to be queen. Choice A is incorrect because the paragraph does not give details about Victoria's childhood. Instead, it talks about her father and other royals. Choice C is incorrect because the next paragraph, paragraph 4, talks about Albert, Victoria's cousin. Choice D is incorrect because only a portion of the paragraph discusses the Duke of Kent. The paragraph is mainly about the royal family as a whole.

26. C: is the correct answer because the paragraph shows that Mrs. Browning predicted that the people would love Victoria and that the people did, ultimately, love her (the paragraph says *there*

are very few sovereigns of whom it could be so truly said that they have been well beloved). Choice A is incorrect because it is the opposite of how the people felt about her. Choice B is incorrect because the quote does not mention Victoria's happiness. Mrs. Browning does predict great happiness, but the paragraph does not say whether or not this prediction came true. Choice D is incorrect because the challenges that Victoria faced are described later in the passage, beginning in paragraph 6.

27. D: is the correct answer because the paragraphs give many details about the troubles that faced the nation when Victoria became queen. Choice A is incorrect because they don't describe what Queen Victoria did to address these problems. Choice B and C are incorrect because the paragraphs discuss these problems and poor conditions as well as many other problems; the purpose of the paragraphs is to describe many problems rather than one specific problem.

28. A: because paragraph 9 states that the system of poor-relief was defective, leading to an immense amount of poverty. Choice B is incorrect because the lack of funding for education was a separate problem from the efforts to aid the poor. Choice C is incorrect because it is not specific and could apply to many of the problems described in paragraphs 7-9. Choice D is incorrect because the government tried to reform the poor-relief system in order to try and solve the problems.

29. B: because paragraph 5 says that Victoria did not know how close she was to the throne until she was twelve years old. This supports the author's point earlier in the sentence that her childhood was simple. Choice A is incorrect because the passage never says she spent time with her cousin; instead, paragraph 4 simply describes Prince Albert's lineage. Choice C is incorrect because Dr. Norman Macleod describes Victoria's independence in 1860, which is well after she becomes an adult. Choice D is incorrect because the passage does not imply that the education caused her childhood to be simple. Instead, the education prepared her for the throne.

30. C: is the correct answer because *tender years* refers to children, or people who are too young to be working. Choice C is the only answer choice that refers to children. Choice A is incorrect because it points out the suffering but does not define *tender years*. Choice B is incorrect for the same reason; *cruelly long* describes the long work hours without defining *tender*. Choice D is incorrect because it refers to women who had to work too hard in the factories. However, *tender years* refers to children who were forced to work.

Writing

1. C: because a comma should not be used to separate the sentence's subject (Paul Revere) and verb (ran). Choice A is incorrect because an apostrophe would make *1760s* possessive, which it is not. Choice B is incorrect because the comma is used to separate a non-essential clause from the rest of the sentence. Choice D is incorrect because the words *busy* and *metalworking* are not a series of adjectives. Instead, *busy* is an adjective modifying the noun *metalworking shop*.

2. C: because *British* is a proper noun and should always be capitalized. Choice A is incorrect because the passage is written in past tense; therefore, *got* should remain in past tense. Choice B is incorrect because it is referring to something getting worse, rather than something that is the superlative *worst*. Choice D is incorrect because *Stamp Act* is both a proper noun and the proper name of the act.

3. A: because a comma should be used to separate the independent clause beginning with *some members* from the non-essential phrase beginning with *which is*. Choice B is incorrect because it is

missing the comma. Choice C is incorrect because it incorrectly uses *that* instead of *which*. Choice D is incorrect because it uses a semicolon instead of a comma.

4. A: because *were* is referring to the plural of *colonists*. As a singular verb form, *was* is incorrect in this case. Choice B is incorrect because *parliament* is the correct spelling. Choice C is incorrect because the comma is required to set off the non-essential phrase that follows. Choice D is incorrect because *that* is used to set off a dependent phrase and should not be preceded by a comma.

5. B: because a comma and conjunction are correctly used to separate two independent clauses. Although choice A has the conjunction *and*, it is missing the required comma. Choice C is incorrect because no comma is required to separate an independent clause from a dependent clause. Choice D is incorrect because the comma creates a run-on sentence.

6. D: "Sonja works very hard" and "she is tired all the time" are both independent clauses (they contain a subject and a verb and express a complete thought). It is appropriate to join two independent clauses with a semicolon. Choice A is a comma splice. Choice B is a run-on sentence. Choice C incorrectly uses a comma to precede the conjunctive adverb "however."

7. A: "Answer" (present tense form of the verb) maintains the parallel structure of the sentence and matches the verb tense of the words "get" and "read." The other answer choices represent the present participle ("answering"), infinitive ("to answer"), and future tense ("will answer").
8. B: The correct spelling of the word is "deleterious."

9. D: a large inscribed stone. A stele is a large, upright stone that typically has writing on it. It is used as a monument; steles were commonly used in ancient cultures in the Middle East.

10. B: mischiefs. This word is not typically used in modern American English; the correct form would be "mischief."

11. D: *from my grandfather, it contained an*
This sentence contains a prepositional phrase and an independent clause separated off the main sentence via semicolon. This is the only choice that uses the correct grammar. A prepositional phrase starts with a preposition and usually ends with a gerund, noun, pronoun, or clause.

12. B: There are basically two ways to live: with your conscience or moral code, which can be a difficult and painful road; or against your conscience, which may seem easy and attractive until you discover how much pain and suffering you've caused others.
A semicolon links two (plus) independent clauses. It can also be used to avoid confusion when listing items. Choice B is listing items and using the semicolon to avoid a misunderstanding. Choices A and C combine a dependent and independent clause. Choice D incorrectly mixes commas and semicolons in the list.

13. C: meticulous. This word should be spelled "meticulous."

14. C: mournful. The meaning of *lachrymose* is *mournful* or *tearful*. This can be the only correct choice because the context of the sentence clearly shows that the girls are distraught (they are crying and comforting each other). They are also talking about an unpleasant subject (bad haircuts).

15. A: Unless you find a new partner

This is an example of a conditional adverbial clause; it acts like an adverb and usually starts with words like *if* or *unless*. This talks about a situation that could happen. The other choices do not make sense in this situation: it's clear from the second part of the sentence that a consequence is coming. Choice B is an independent clause, Choice C is a time clause, and Choice D is a clause of manner.

16. A: I packed a picnic to take to the park with my friends; I made sure that I brought all of the plates and cups, too.

A semicolon is used to connect two independent clauses that are closely related. A comma should not be used to separate independent clauses as a comma is more for a pause in the text. The sentence needs some punctuation, so Choice C is incorrect. Choice D uses a colon, which should be used to show a list or provide an explanation.

17. B: sureptitious

This word should be spelled with 2 *r*'s: surreptitious. It means something that is secret or sly.

18. C: rancorous. *Acrimonious* means "bitter" or "vitriolic," and is very similar in meaning to *rancorous*.

19. B: To defer is to temporarily put off, postpone, or delay an action. To defer a loan is to postpone its repayment with the intention of resuming repayments in the future. To decry means to criticize. To differ means to vary or disagree. Debtor is a noun meaning someone who owes a debt.

20. B: interpretation, evolution, interpret. This question deals with being able to identify different meanings or parts of speech through patterns in words. The first and second blanks refer to nouns; the third blank is a verb. Choice A provides noun, verb, verb. Choice C provides verb, noun, noun. Choice D provides all nouns.

21. B: The sentence compares the melody of a pop song to that of the first movement in Beethoven's ninth symphony. Therefore, concluding that they probably are similar is logical. The pop song reminds the speaker of the Beethoven piece, which means the pop song suggests the melody of the Beethoven piece. Reminiscent and suggestive are synonyms in this context.

22. A: This sentence offers the most effective revision. The syntax is clearer than the other answer choices. The writer achieves maximum impact by holding Mary Shelley's achievement, the creation of Dr. Frankenstein and his hideous monster in her novel Frankenstein, for the end of the sentence.

23. C: The Merriam-Webster's Dictionary states that \im-'präm(p)-(,)tü is the correct pronunciation of the word "impromptu." This pronunciation indicates that the o is pronounced ä, which is an open vowel that sounds like "ah," the p is optional, and the
ü is pronounced "oo."

24. B: This is the most effective revision. The syntax is clearer than the original sentence and it retains the vivid description of automobile as a "friend and foe." The other choices either are confusingly structured or ordinarily worded.

25. C: The first statement establishes the idea that repairing route 211 will have financial consequences on the community. The correct answer choice supports this statement by providing specific figures regarding the amount of money the potholes in route 211 cost drivers last year. The

other answer choices may be relevant in the argument, but they do not follow the statement in the question as well.

26. C: A word's origin, or etymology, will give you a clue to its meaning. A brass ring merely gilded with gold, a fawney, is hardly the same thing as a solid gold ring. Attempting to pass of such a ring as pure gold would be untruthful and the ring would only be a fake gold ring. The words phony and fake share the same meaning. Although fawning sounds and looks similar to fawney, the former means flattering or submissive, which provides no indication of the real meaning of fawney.

27. D: The context of the sentence indicates that Mara would feel great happiness.

28. D: Although the word choices all have similar denotations, the context of the sentence, and especially the use of the word "grudgingly," indicate that Stanley gave only a perfunctory congratulations to Nathan for his good idea. The sentence should read: Stanley had never liked Nathan, but he grudgingly commended Nathan for his idea of holding a car wash for the school fund raiser.

29. D: "Hunting down the truth" is a figure of speech that means "determined to learn the truth." This is indicated by the context of the sentence which references the life goal of a detective.

30. A: This sentence best conveys the information without using too many words or having an awkward construction (choices B, C, and D).